HANGUL
FROM ZERO!

George Trombley

Reed Bullen

Jiyoon Kim

Myunghee Ham

© 2014-2023 All Rights Reserved, From Zero, LLC.

Hangul From Zero!
The Complete Guide to Learning Korean Writing including 250 vocabulary!

PREFACE
Hangul From Zero! is part of the Korean language book series "Korean From Zero!". Many students learn Korean from other Korean learning sources. For this reason we have separated the Hangul lessons from Korean From Zero! book 1 into this separate updated volume. We hope your Korean studies advance with the added content not available in our other lessons.

DEDICATION
This book is dedicated and made for people who truly want to learn Korean and the Korean writing system, *hangul*, also spelled *hangeul*, but it's also written for:

Korean culture lovers, Korean drama watchers, Korean beginners, KPOP music fans, BTS and or Stray Kids stans, people of Korean heritage connecting to their history, and anyone planning travel to Korea! Because without being able to read Korean, your access to the culture of Korea and it's many offerings will be much more limited.

All of us on the *Korean From Zero!* and *Hangul From Zero!* team wish you success on your road to Korean fluency.

DISTRIBUTION

Distributed in the USA & Canada by:
From Zero LLC.
10624 S. Eastern Ave. #A769
Henderson, NV 89052, USA
sales@fromzero.com

Distributed in the UK & Europe by:
Bay Language Books Ltd.
Unit 4, Kingsmead, Park Farm, Folkestone,
Kent. CT19 5EU, Great Britain
sales@baylanguagebooks.co.uk

COPYRIGHT
Copyright © 2014-2023 From Zero, LLC. All Rights Reserved.
Printed in USA / England / Australia
ISBN-10: 0996786309
ISBN-13: 978-0-9967863-0-0

1st edition, January 2023

Hangul From Zero! – Korean Writing Book

- ❑ How this book works: Welcome! 5
- ❑ The Start: Introduction to Hangul 9
- ❑ Korean Reading and Writing: Creating Simple Hangul 11
- ❑ Korean Reading and Writing: Pure Vowel Sounds 23
- ❑ Korean Reading and Writing: Hard Hangul Sounds 35
- ❑ Korean Reading and Writing: Double Consonants 45
- ❑ Korean Reading and Writing: Final Consonants 55
- ❑ Korean Reading and Writing: Sound Change Rules 64
- ❑ Korean Reading and Writing: Typing Hangul 71
- ❑ 250 Korean Vocabulary Words in Hangul 76
- ❑ Map of South Korea 163
- ❑ Hangul Character Name Chart 164
- ❑ Korean Keyboard Layout 166
- ❑ Korean Keyboard Layout 168
- ❑ Other From Zero! Books 170

You can help with a book review!

Reviews help! Please visit any of the major book seller websites and post a review of *Hangul From Zero!* We are fanatical about making the best books for students who don't have access to a Korean teacher. Your book reviews help make new books possible and make us smile!

You can help with feedback!

If you love (we hope), hate (we are sad), or are confused (sorry!) about any concept in this book please email as at **feedback@fromzero.com** with your feedback so we can improve future versions.

VISIT **KoreanFromZero.com**!

Support for your Korean Learning!
- Mobile and Browser Audio Anytime Streaming
- FULL AUDIO sound pack for PC and MAC
- Free Flashcard Download and Other Materials

Thank you and enjoy your Korean journey,

The entire From Zero! team

How this book works:
Welcome!

 Getting Started

❑ **Play the sounds on mobile and in the browser!**
To listen to the audio files on your mobile device or in any browser visit:
MOBILE / PC: http://koreanfromzero.com/hangul
DOWNLOAD: http://koreanfromzero.com/audio-hangul
WORKBOOK AUDIO: http://koreanfromzero.com/hangul

❑ **Download the sound pack!**
Visit **koreanfromzero.com/audio-hangul** and download the Free Audio Files.

STEP 1: Download the zipped audio file to your WINDOWS or MAC computer.

STEP 2: Unzip (uncompress) the zipped file.

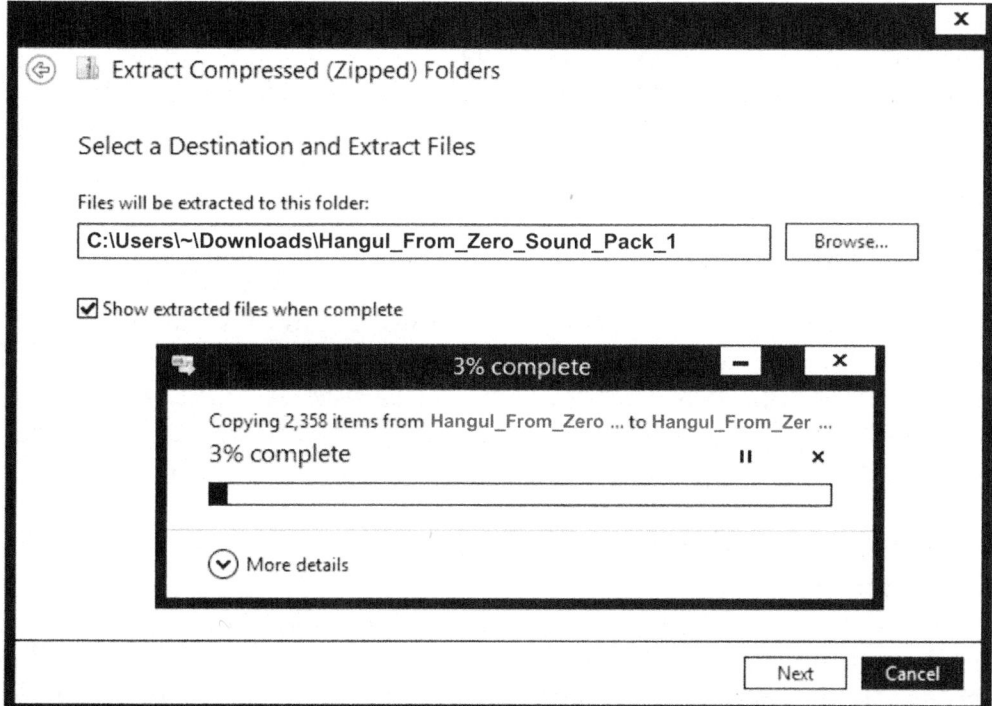

Introduction

❑ Welcome to HANGUL FROM ZERO!

WHAT ARE THESE CIRCLES, LINES, AND SQUARES? The Korean language uses a set of symbols called *Hangul* (한글, pronounced hangool), to spell all words in the Korean language. In the past, *hanja*, Chinese characters, were heavily used in Korea, but in modern Korea you can get by without ever learning very much - if any - *hanja*. In the first book, we will give you a crash course in *Hangul*. It is said that *Hangul* can be learned in a day but takes years to master. Throughout the lessons we will reinforce what is taught in the *Hangul* lessons and teach you exceptions to the rules, such as specific sound changes, as needed. NOTE: *Hangul* is sometimes spelled "hangeul" to match the official Korean Romanization. We chose "hangul" since it it best matches western spelling expectation, but both are used.

❑ Korean punctuation facts

HERE ARE SOME QUICK FACTS about Korean writing to help you get started.

UPPERCASE/LOWERCASE
In English, we learn to write both *A* and *a*, but in Korean there are no upper and lower cases. In other words, 아 is always 아 no matter where you find it in a sentence.
SENTENCE ENDING PUNCTUATION
Written Korean uses question marks, exclamation points, commas, and periods just like English. You will see their usage throughout the book.

❑ Before grammar…

The best thing you can do, for your Korean, is learn how to read Korean well. This is not a choice. You MUST learn *Hangul*. Once you know how to read, you will learn many key Korean grammar concepts that will set you firmly on the path to fluency. Many of the best Korean resources for learning are only available in *Hangul*. If you want to watch KDRAMA without subtitles, or sing your favorite KPOP song at a Korean karaoke room without constantly looking at the lyrics on your phone, then learning *Hangul* is a MUST!

❑ About the authors

George Trombley
Author George Trombley is a professional Japanese interpreter and author of the "Japanese From Zero!" book series. For over 20+ years he has interpreted at corporations such as Microsoft, IBM, NTT DoCoMo, Lucent Technologies,

Varian Medical and in countries throughout North America, Europe, Asia and the Middle East. For "Korean From Zero!" series, George has teamed up his co-authors to create books that are accessible for beginners, yet deep enough to help students of Korean at any level.

Reed Bullen
Reed learned Korean initially for his missionary work in South Korea. During his stay in Korea he lived in Daejeon and met hundreds of Koreans, volunteered for farm work, and worked with local Korean orphanages. After his mission he continued studying Korean. He has now co-authored, including this book, four Korean textbooks.

Jiyoon Kim (Katie Kim)
Jiyoon grew up in Seoul and graduated from UNLV with a degree in hospitality management. She was a natural choice to join the *Korean From Zero!* team and has been instrumental in designing the sentences and debating the grammar that make up the series. Jiyoon brings a special perspective that the other authors don't share since she learned English as a second language and isn't classically trained in teaching Korean.

Myunghee Ham
Myunghee Ham attended college at Myongji university and has a degree in Korean literature and is also fluent in Japanese. She has been teaching Korean to foreigners for over 8 years, and currently works as a Korean teacher at Seoul Korean language academy.

❑ WRITE IN THIS BOOK!
This book is your tool to <u>learning in a way that will stick!</u> Learning Korean is hard work so we want your knowledge to last forever. *Hangul From Zero!* is designed to be an <u>interactive workbook</u> where you can develop your writing skills from hopeless/crazy/illegible (we all start that way!) to expert-level.

Every time you write in this book, you're making your connection to Korean a little bit stronger.

화이팅! (hwaiting!)

*Koreans say this to mean, "persevere". It comes from the English word "fighting".

George Trombley, Reed Bullen, Jiyoon Kim, Myunghee Ham

The Start: Introduction to Hangul

Why Learn Hangul?

Hangul is the main writing system of Korea. It's famous for being easy to learn and in many linguistic circles is considered genius. Prior to its invention in the 15th century, Korean used the same Chinese characters as China and Japan. Japanese and Chinese children spend a significant part of the school years devoted to learning the often complicated Chinese characters, but hangul can be learned in a few days for an average adult.

Hanja
Over 5000 characters for Chinese and 2000 for Japanese are used commonly.

Korean Hangul
Just 24 unique symbols combine to make 12,000+ Hangul combinations.

If you aren't convinced yet as to how cool hangul is, here are the top five reasons you should learn hangul:

1. **It's easy. WAY easier than you imagine!**
   Some people say you can learn it in just two hours.

2. **It's cool. Seriously… none of your friends can write it!**
   Unless your friends are all studying Korean or ARE Korean you will be the coolest person around when you say, and show them, that you can read and write Korean!

3. **Your accent improves.**
   You have spent much of your life reading Roman letters (ABC) in a certain way. If you learn Korean with those letters you will often still read them the

same way and not have a great Korean accent. If you learn hangul, you won't have to fight your English speaking habits!

4. **Korean Romanization can be a bit confusing. Hangul is just easier!**
With combinations like "SEO" and "SAE" and "SEU" it's pretty easy to screw up the Romanization of Korean. Hangul fixes this problem. Besides… imagine if a Korean person decided to learn English only using hangul characters!

5. **There is no choice!**
Because hangul is so easy, it's rare that a book teaching Korean teaches using Roman letters. The entire "Korean From Zero!" series does not use Romanization.

Hangul Consonants and Vowels

Hangul characters are "built" using consonant and vowel parts. Using these individual parts over 12,000 characters can be constructed.

Don't worry about memorizing the chart on this page, it's mainly to be used as a reference. This book will gradually teach you to read and write hangul.

Consonants: single key on keyboard

ㄱ	ㄴ	ㄷ	ㄹ	ㅁ	ㅂ	ㅅ	ㅇ	ㅈ	ㅊ	ㅋ	ㅌ	ㅍ	ㅎ
G	N	D	R/L	M	B	S	null/NG	J	CH	K	T	P	H

Consonants: double key on keyboard (shift + consonant)

ㅃ	ㅉ	ㄸ	ㄲ	ㅆ
PP	JJ	DD	KK	SS

Vowels: single key on keyboard

ㅏ	ㅑ	ㅓ	ㅕ	ㅗ	ㅛ	ㅜ	ㅠ	ㅡ	ㅣ	ㅐ	ㅔ
a	ya	eo	yeo	o	yo	u	yu	eu	i	ae	e

Vowels: double key on keyboard (shift OR vowel + vowel)

ㅒ	ㅖ	ㅘ	ㅙ	ㅚ	ㅝ	ㅞ	ㅟ	ㅢ
yae	ye	wa	wae	woe	wo	we	wi	ui

A Korean Reading and Writing: Creating Simple Hangul

A New Hangul

In this lesson we will focus on the first five consonants and five vowels. Writing with the correct stroke order will make your writing neater.

Consonants

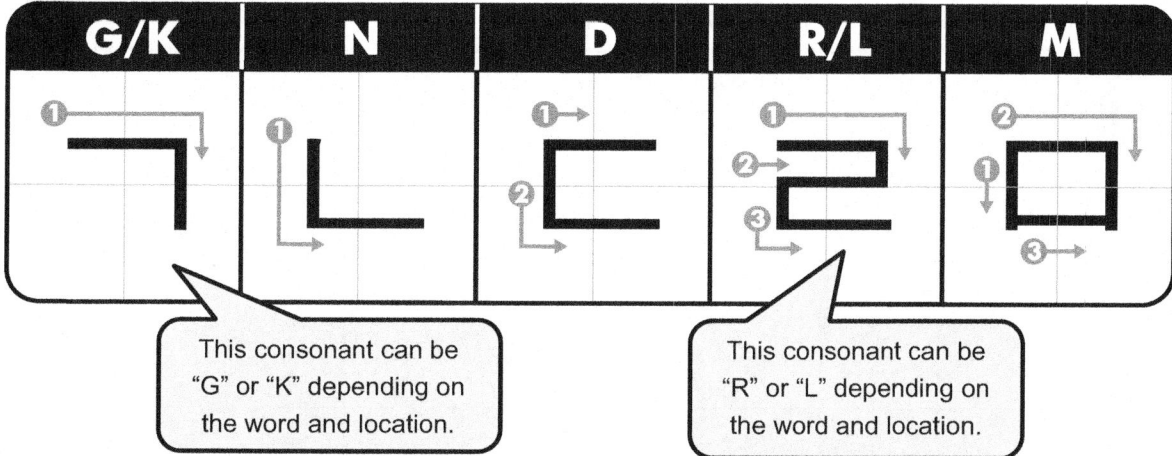

This consonant can be "G" or "K" depending on the word and location.

This consonant can be "R" or "L" depending on the word and location.

Practice writing by first tracing the gray, then writing on your own.

Vowels

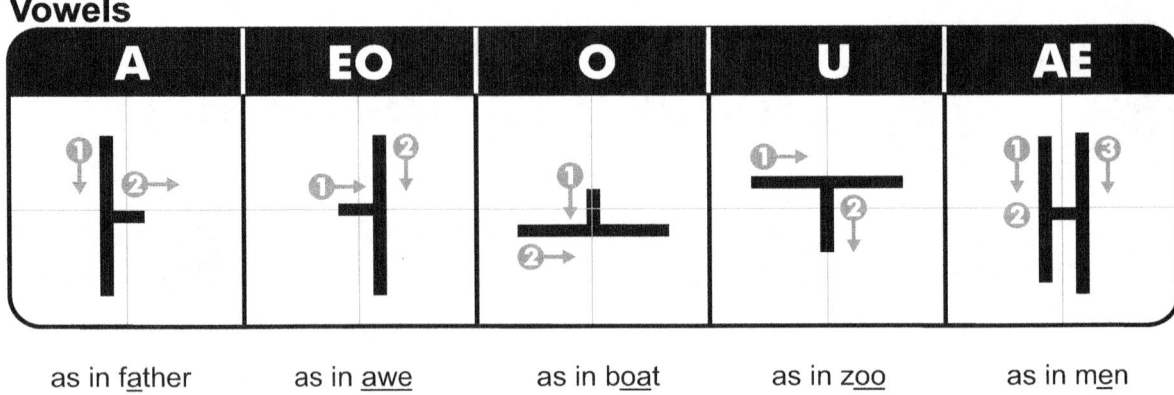

A	EO	O	U	AE
as in f**a**ther	as in **awe**	as in b**oa**t	as in z**oo**	as in m**e**n

Practice writing by first tracing the gray, then writing on your own.

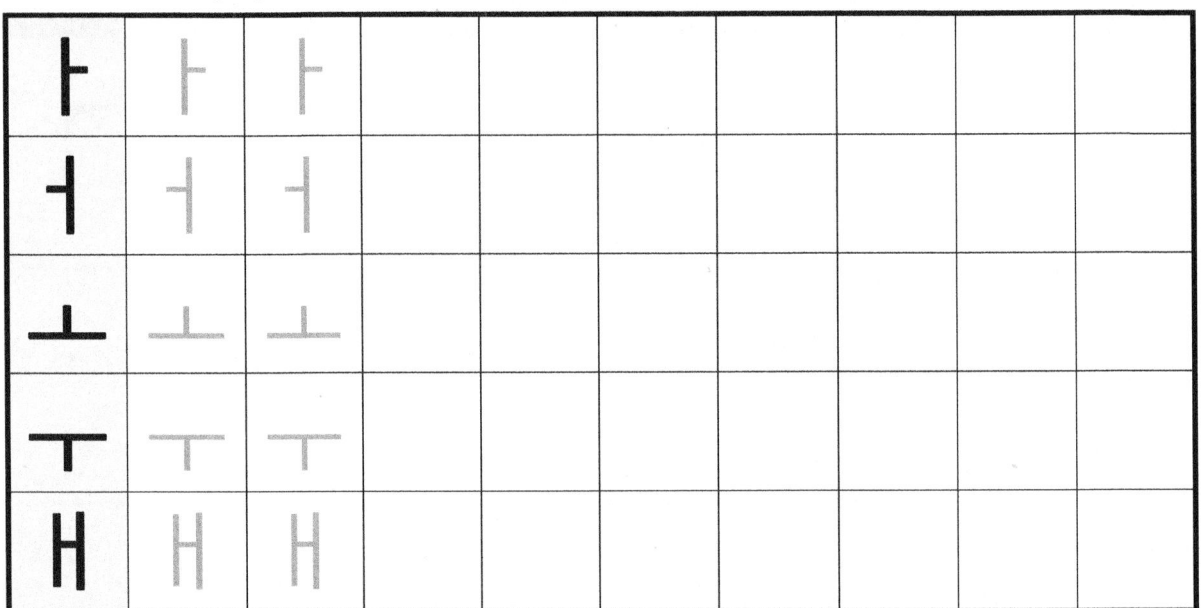

A | Hangul Facts

Before King Sejong invented the hangul phonetic system, only the elite were able to read and write Korean. Koreans still study around 1800 Hanja (Chinese characters) through high school.

When learning Japanese or Chinese it can take many years to learn the thousands of characters, and even then you will often run into characters you haven't learned yet. Hangul has made it possible for anyone, including foreigners to easily learn to read and write Korean in just a few days.

Even though you might not understand what you are reading, after learning hangul you will be able to read any book you pick up in Korea, from comic books to full blown novels.

A | Hangul Usage

❑ A-1. Using consonants and vowels to create sounds

You can never just write a consonant or vowel alone. Instead you will combine consonants and vowels to make a hangul sound character.
For example ㅁ (M) + ㅏ (A) makes 마 (MA).

When creating a sound you will always start with a consonant, and then follow it with a vowel. Let's look at some simple consonant + vowel combinations:

g	a	ga		d	a	da
ㄱ	+ ㅏ	= 가		ㄷ	+ ㅏ	= 다

n	a	na		r	a	ra
ㄴ	+ ㅏ	= 나		ㄹ	+ ㅏ	= 라

Practice writing the new sounds. Trace the gray items first.

가	가						
나	나						
다	다						
라	라						
마	마						

A-2. Writing order and orientation

There are standing (vertical) and laying (horizontal) vowels. Standing vowels always "stand" to the right of the consonant. Laying vowels always "lay" below the consonant.

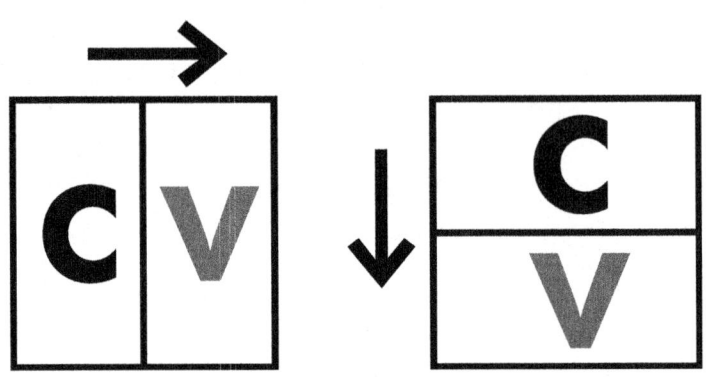

left / right combinations

ga	ge	na	ne	da	de	ra	re	ma	me
가	개	나	내	다	대	라	래	마	매

top / bottom combinations

go	gu	no	nu	do	du	ro	ru	mo	mu
고	구	노	누	도	두	로	루	모	무

Practice writing the left / right combination sounds. Trace the gray first.

거	거				개	개			
너	너				내	내			
더	더				대	대			
러	러				래	래			
머	머				매	매			

Practice writing the top / bottom combination sounds. Trace the gray first.

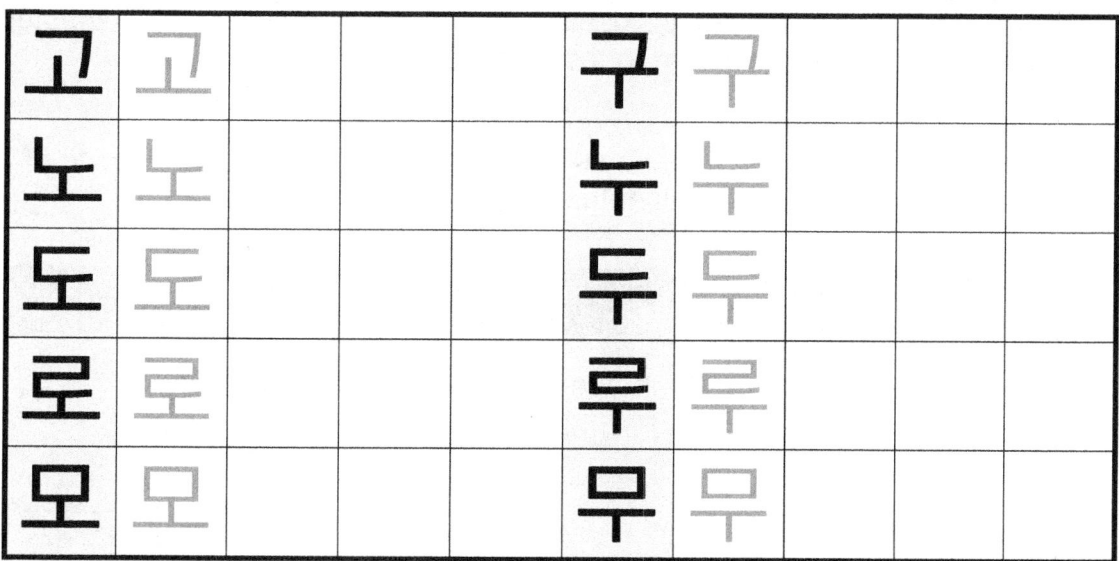

❏ A-3. The different sounds of ㄱ, ㄹ

ㄱ can be pronounced like a G or a K. Typically at the beginning of a sentence or word you will hear ㄱ like a K, and if it is in the middle of a word it's closer to a G.

ㄹ can be pronounced like an R or an L. Typically at the beginning of a sentence you will hear ㄹ like a R and in the middle more like L.

As you learn Korean you will find that, depending on the word, the sound of ㄱ and ㄹ will shift. In many cases you just have to learn how that particular word is pronounced.

❏ A-4. The sound difference between ㅓ and ㅗ

The sound for ㅓ doesn't really exist in English so it might be hard to master. One technique to getting closer to the right sound is this trick:

1. Open your mouth as if you are going to say "AH"
2. Now say "OH". It should feel as if the sound is coming from the back of your throat. Your mouth will naturally close as you try to say "OH".

A | Writing Practice

First trace the light gray characters, then write each character 10 times.

ga	가									
na	나									
no	노									
da	다									
do	도									
reo	러									
ru	루									
mae	매									
mo	모									
geo	거									
ma	마									

Hangul From Zero! – Lesson A – Creating Simple Hangul   **17**

A | Words You Can Write

Using just the hangul from this lesson, we can already write many Korean words.

개
dog

다
everything, all

가구
furniture

나라
country

노래
song

누구
who

도마
cutting board

모래
sand

매너
manners

모두
everyone

누나
older sister (when said by males)

고구마
sweet potato

A | Hangul Matching

Connect the dots between each hangul and the correct Romanization. You can check your answers in the Answer Key at the end of this lesson.

매 ·		· reo
다 ·		· do
도 ·		· gu
루 ·		· ma
마 ·		· mae
내 ·		· ru
러 ·		· da
고 ·		· go
구 ·		· nae

A | Listening Quiz

For this section you will need to listen to the audio provided for free at:
http://koreanfromzero.com/hangul/

❏ AA-1. Listen and Choose

Listen to the sounds in **Lesson A > Listening Quiz 1** then circle what you hear.

1	① 가	② 나	5	① 고	② 도
2	① 머	② 모	6	① 래	② 내
3	① 루	② 로	7	① 마	② 다
4	① 매	② 대	8	① 로	② 러

❑ AA-2. Listen and Write

Listen to the sound in **Lesson A > Listening Quiz 2** and write down the hangul sounds you hear in the exact order that you hear them in.

1	2	3	4	5	6	7	8	9	10

❑ AA-3. Listen and Number

Listen to the eight words in the sound file in **Lesson A > Listening Quiz 3**, then on the line below, number each word 1-8 underneath in the order that the words are spoken.

A | Lesson Answer Key

❏ Hangul Matching (answers)

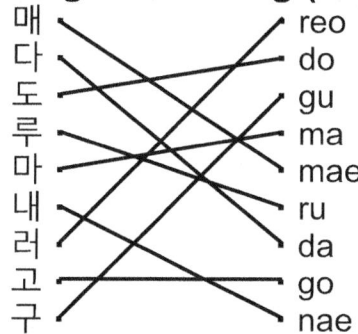

❏ AA-1. Listen and Choose (answers)

1	② 나	5	② 도
2	② 모	6	① 래
3	① 루	7	① 마
4	② 대	8	② 러

❏ AA-2. Listen and Write (answers)

1	2	3	4	5	6	7	8	9	10
래	도	러	가	마	거	루	다	대	모

❏ AA-3. Listen and Number (answers)

가구	도마	누나	노래
6	2	7	4
모두	모래	누구	나라
1	3	8	5

A | Hangul Practice Boxes

Use these boxes to practice writing the hangul you learned in lesson A.

B Korean Reading and Writing: Pure Vowel Sounds

B New Hangul

Let's learn five more consonants and five more vowels.

Consonants

Practice writing by first tracing the gray, then writing on your own.

Vowels

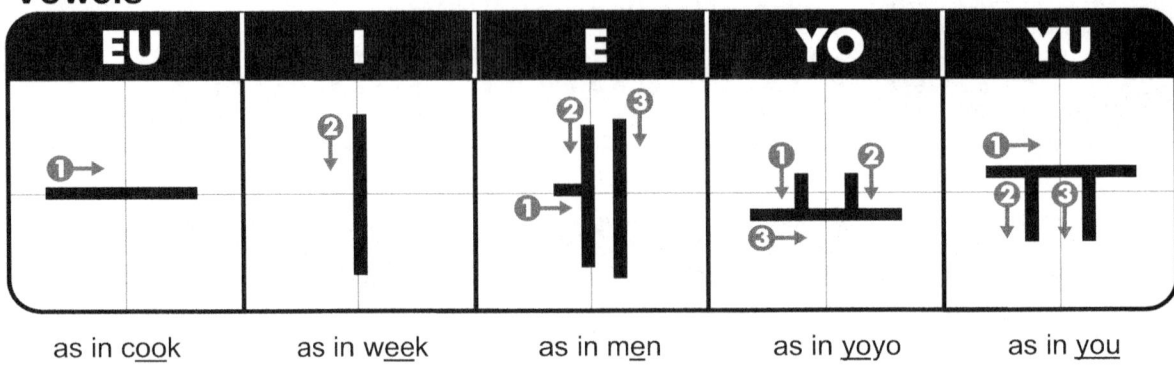

Practice writing by first tracing the gray, then writing on your own.

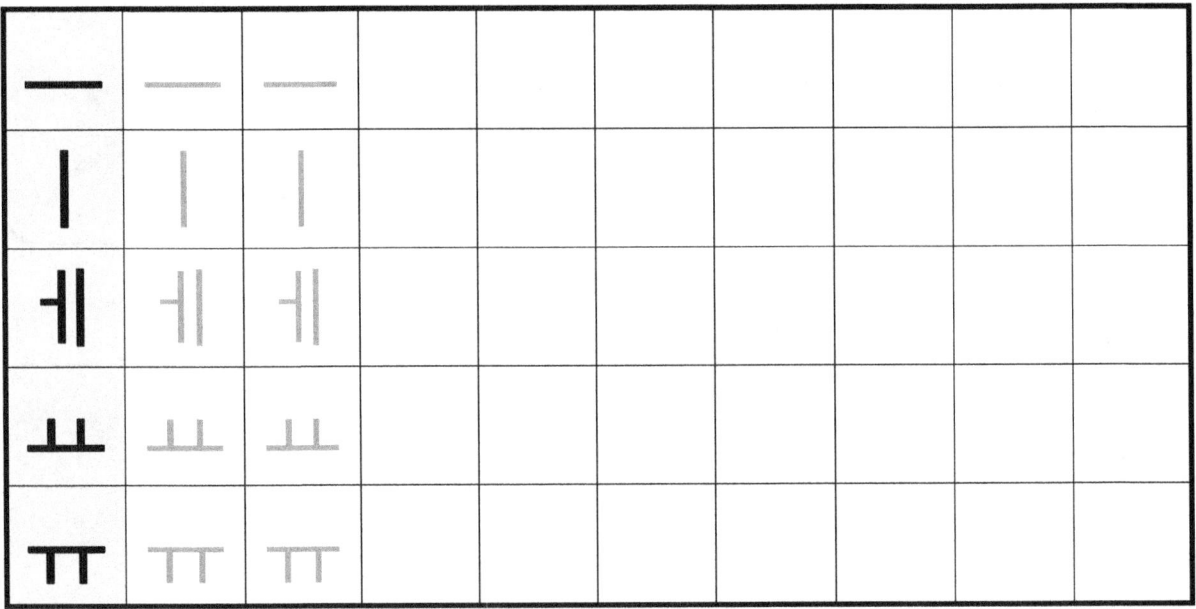

B | Hangul Facts

Did you know that hangul isn't only used in Korea? According to a report from the Yonhap News Agency, in August 2009 a minority tribe in Indonesia chose hangul as it's official writing system.

The tribe has a population of 60,000 and was on the verge of losing its native language as it lacked a proper writing system. This is the first time hangul has been used for another language.

B | Hangul Usage

❑ B-1. Creating pure vowels with ㅇ

In this lesson we introduce the hangul character ㅇ. In order to say a pure vowel, meaning a vowel all by itself, you must use ㅇ in the consonant spot. Here are some examples:

아 (a)　　　이 (i)　　　오 (o)　　　애 (ae)

You MUST start a pure vowel with ㅇ. In other words, you can never have a vowel by itself. When ㅇ is the first character then it is silent and makes no sound.

Notice how the orientation of the ㅇ changes depending on the vowel it's used with. The shape of the ㅇ doesn't have to change, but many Korean fonts change the shape for balance reasons.

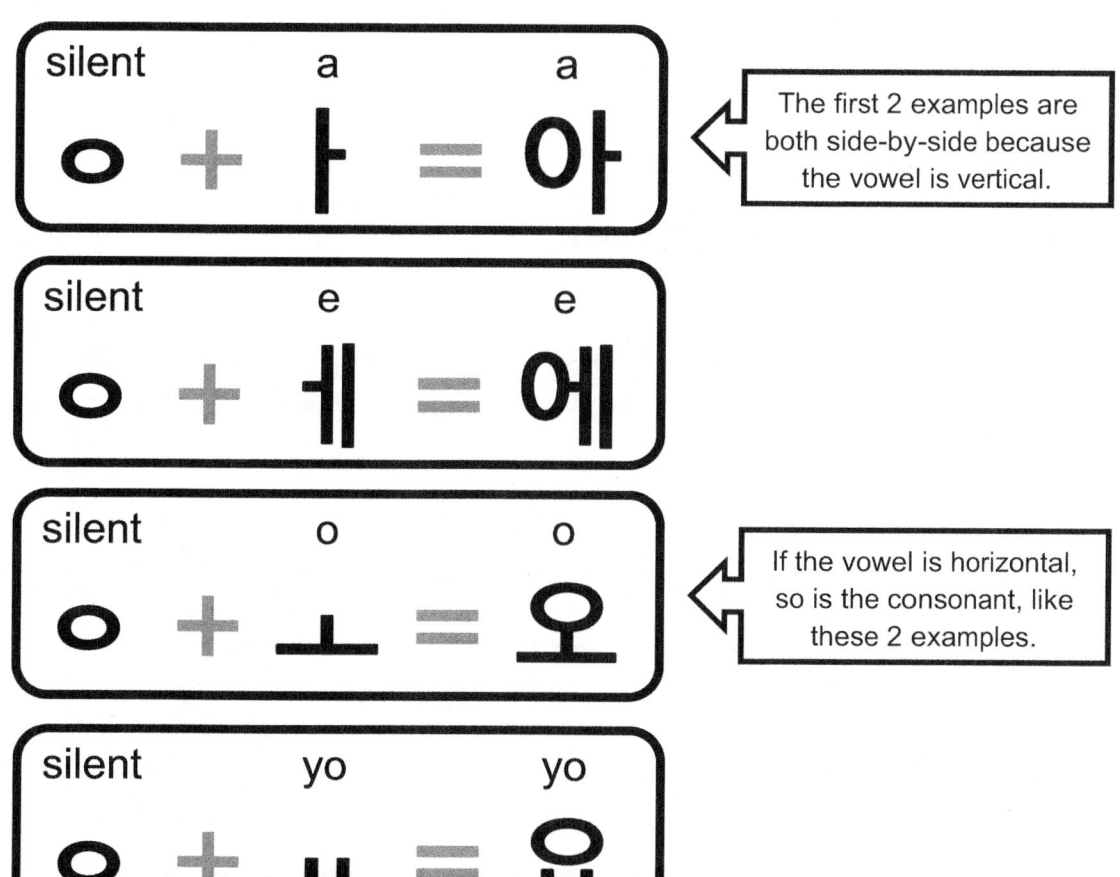

Here are some example words using the hangul you have already learned.
See if you can read them.

아이	child
요리	cooking
우유	milk
어디	where
이유	reason
아기	baby
오다	to come
이	teeth

❑ B-2. Written versions versus font versions of hangul

When you first learn hangul you might be confused as to how some characters change when written versus when typed. Let's look at how ㅈ and ㅊ change when written.

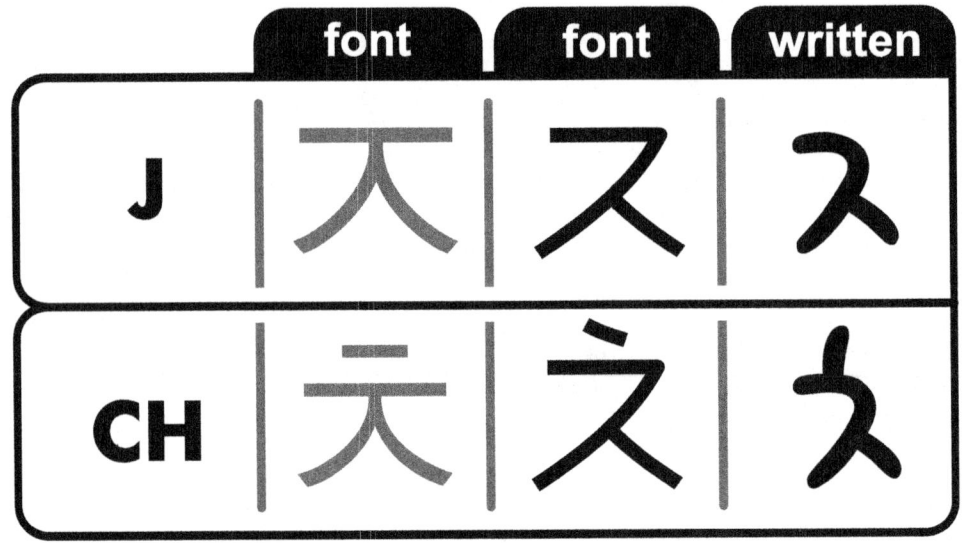

❑ B-3. The different sounds of ㅅ

ㅅ normally sounds like an "S" sound, however when combined with certain hangul it will sound like an "SH" sound. We cover this rule in Lesson G.

NOTE: When ㅛ (yo) and ㅠ (yu) are combined the "y" is discarded in the Romanization.

said as "S"	said as "SH"
사 (sa)	시 (shi)
서 (seo)	쇼 (sho)
소 (so)	슈 (shu)
새 (sae)	셔 (sheo)
세 (se)	샤 (sha)
수 (su)	
스 (seu)	

ㅕ and ㅑ vowels are introduced in the next lesson.

❑ B-4. The difference between ㅐ and ㅔ

In modern Korea, there is no easily distinguished sound difference between ㅐ and ㅔ vowels.

Some words use one or the other based on the roots of the word. You simply just need to learn how to "spell" some words in Korean, just like in English.

세대	generation
새매	sparrow hawk
베이지	beige
배우	actor, actress

❑ B-5. The difference between ㅜ and ㅡ

To the untrained ear these will both sound the same. But the mouth makes a different shape for ㅜ and ㅡ.

ㅜ is said with the lips pushed out like you're trying to kiss someone and saying "oo" as in "moon".

ㅡ is said by pulling the lips back almost as far as you can and saying the same "oo" sound.

B | Writing Practice

First trace the light gray characters, then write each character 10 times.

beu	브											
bi	비											
se	세											
ji	지											
byo	뵤											
yo	요											

Hangul From Zero! – Lesson B – Pure Vowel Sounds

a	아										
shi	시										
shu	슈										
chae	채										
jeo	저										
eu	으										

B Words You Can Write

Using just the hangul from this lesson, we can already write many Korean words.

비
rain

시
poem

차
car

버스
bus

세대
generation

아기 — baby

주스 — juice

자유 — freedom, liberty

개미 — ant

베개 — pillow

다시 — again, one more time

부츠 — boots

고기 — meat

B | Hangul Matching

Connect the dots between each hangul and the correct Romanization. You can check your answers in the Answer Key at the end of this lesson.

시 ·		· jeo
슈 ·		· shi
오 ·		· che
체 ·		· ja
브 ·		· se
요 ·		· shu
자 ·		· beu
저 ·		· o
세 ·		· yo

B | Listening Quiz

For this section you will need to listen to the audio provided for free at:
http://koreanfromzero.com/hangul/

❏ BA-1. Listen and Choose

Listen to the sounds in **Lesson B > Listening Quiz 1** then circle what you hear.

1	① 비	② 디	5	① 자	② 차
2	① 아	② 어	6	① 요	② 오
3	① 슈	② 쇼	7	① 마	② 바
4	① 스	② 시	8	① 수	② 소

❏ BA-2. Listen and Write

Listen to the sound in **Lesson B > Listening Quiz 2** and write down the hangul sounds you hear in the exact order that you hear them in.

1	2	3	4	5	6	7	8	9	10

❏ BA-3. Listen and Number

Listen to the eight words in the sound file in **Lesson B > Listening Quiz 3**, then on the line below, number each word 1-8 underneath in the order that the words are spoken.

Hangul From Zero! – Lesson B – Pure Vowel Sounds

B | Lesson Answer Key

❏ Hangul Matching (answers)

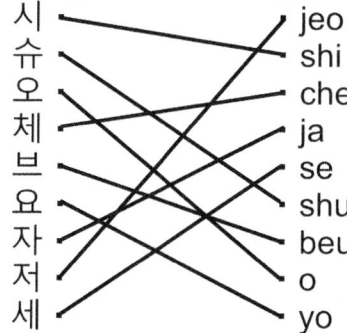

❏ BA-1. Listen and Choose (answers)

1	① 비	5	② 차
2	② 어	6	① 요
3	② 쇼	7	② 바
4	① 스	8	① 수

❏ BA-2. Listen and Write (answers)

1	2	3	4	5	6	7	8	9	10
아	어	비	제	슈	죠	치	기	요	러

❏ BA-3. Listen and Number (answers)

아이	개미	세대	주스
6	1	8	7
어디	우유	배우	고기
5	2	4	3

B | Hangul Practice Boxes

Use these boxes to practice writing the hangul you learned in lesson B.

Hangul From Zero! – Lesson C – Hard Hangul Sounds   **35**

Korean Reading and Writing:
Hard Hangul Sounds

C | New Hangul

In this lesson we learn four more consonants and five more vowels.

Consonants

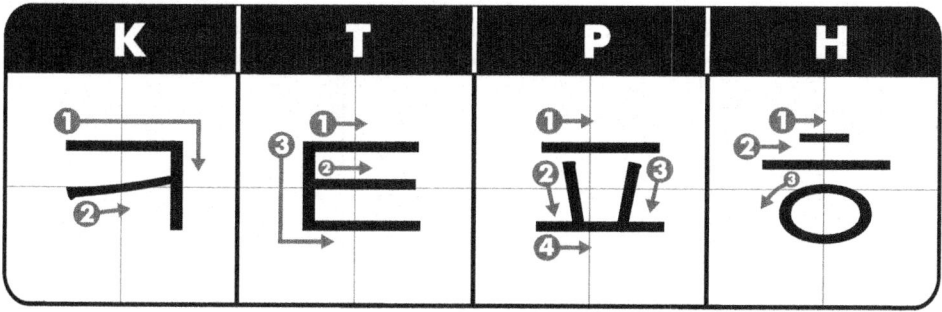

Practice writing by first tracing the gray, then writing on your own.

ㅋ	ㅋ	ㅋ						
ㅌ	ㅌ	ㅌ						
ㅍ	ㅍ	ㅍ						
ㅎ	ㅎ	ㅎ						

Vowels

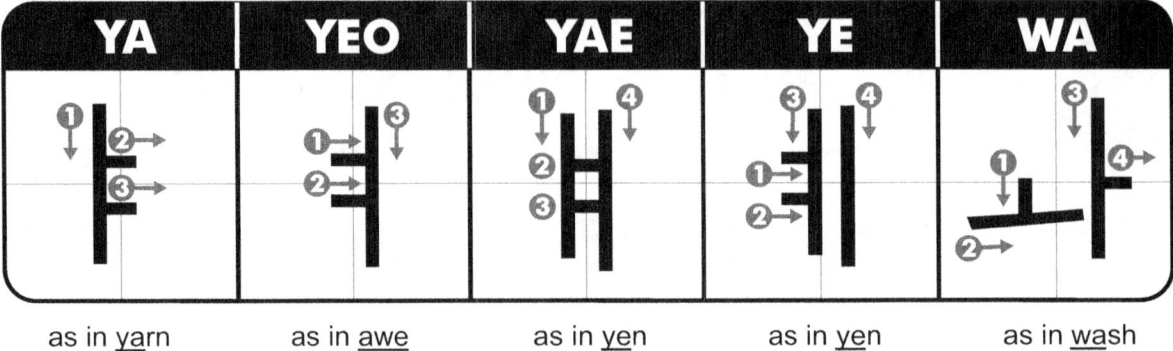

YA	YEO	YAE	YE	WA
as in <u>ya</u>rn	as in <u>aw</u>e	as in <u>ye</u>n	as in <u>ye</u>n	as in <u>wa</u>sh

Practice writing by first tracing the gray, then writing on your own.

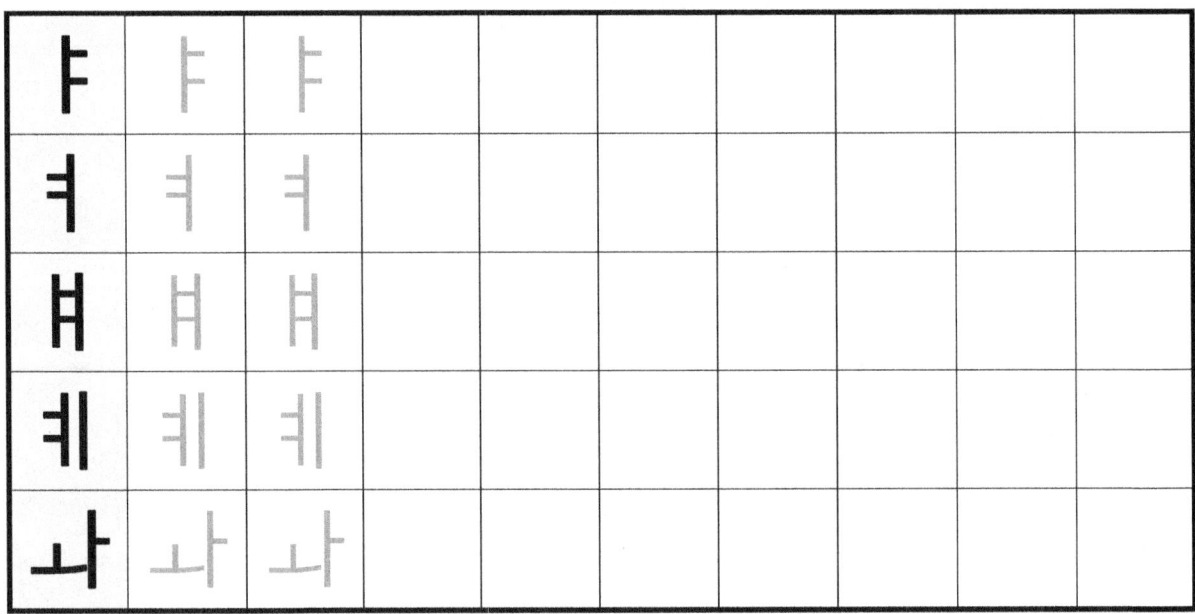

C | Hangul Facts

North Korea and South Korea both use hangul for their writing systems however after the Korean war, several laws changed the way Korean was spoken in both countries. One big difference is that words in South Korea that started with 리 were changed to all start with 이. The word "reason" in North Korea is pronounced 리유, but in the South it's pronounced 이유.

Even the names of each of the hangul characters are different between each country.

C | Hangul Usage

❏ C-1. Hard and soft sounds with Hangul
ㅂ, ㄷ, ㅈ, and ㄱ can have "soft" and a "hard" sounds.

ㅂ	ㅂ is "B", but there are cases where it also sounds like a "P".
ㄷ	ㄷ is "D", but in some cases it will be "T".
ㅈ	ㅈ is "J" but sometimes it's "CH".
ㄱ	ㄱ is "G", but in some cases it will sound like "K".

In the beginning of a word ㅂ, ㄷ, ㅈ, and ㄱ will tend to be "stronger" sounds like P, T, CH, and K. But will be softer in the middle and end of words.

ㅍ (P), ㅌ (T), ㅊ (CH), ㅋ (K) are ALWAYS pronounced with hard sounds. Listen to the sounds of the following words to hear the differences.

피트	feet (measurement)
비드	bead
코치	coach
고지	notification

❏ C-2. The difference between ㅐ and ㅔ
ㅐ and ㅔ are both pronounced like the "ye" in "yen". In modern Korean they are the same sound. Consider them just different ways of spelling.

예 (ye)	애 (yae)

예보	forcast (weather)
애기	story

❑ C-3. Vowel sound overlap when used with consonants.

In section C-3 we learned that ㅐ ㅖ and pronounced as "ye". However when these vowels are used with a consonant most Koreans will pronounce them the same as ㅔ and ㅐ.

| 게 (ge) | 개 (gae) | 계 (gye) | 걔 (gyae) |

Despite different vowels these "g" sounds are all pronounced the same.

개 — dog
게 — crab
걔 — he/she
세계 — the world

❑ C-4. Written and typed versions of ㅎ

ㅎ (H), looks different depending on the font and penmanship.

C — Writing Practice

First trace the light gray characters, then write each character 10 times.

ko	코									
teu	트									
pa	파									

Hangul From Zero! – Lesson C – Hard Hangul Sounds   39

ha	하										
sha	샤										
gyeo	겨										
wa	와										
gye	계										
teo	터										
gwa	과										
ryeo	려										

C | Words You Can Write

Using just the hangul from this lesson, we can already write many Korean words.

코
nose

| 코 | | | | | | | | | | | |

화
anger

| 화 | | | | | | | | | | | |

타다
to ride

| 타 | 다 | | | | | | | | | | |

피
blood

| 피 | | | | | | | | | | | |

Korean	English
세계	the world
파티	party
피자	pizza
노트	notebook
애기	story, talk
그녀	her, she
야채	vegetables
커피	coffee
히터	heater

Hangul From Zero! – Lesson C – Hard Hangul Sounds

C | Hangul Matching

Connect the dots between each hangul and the correct Romanization. You can check your answers in the Answer Key at the end of this lesson.

히 ·	· teu
파 ·	· pa
와 ·	· hi
커 ·	· yae
트 ·	· gye
애 ·	· keo
랴 ·	· rya
계 ·	· hwa
화 ·	· wa

C | Listening Quiz

For this section you will need to listen to the audio provided for free at:
http://koreanfromzero.com/hangul/

❑ **CA-1. Listen and Choose**
Listen to the sounds in **Lesson C > Listening Quiz 1** then circle what you hear.

1	① 쿄	② 교	5	① 촤	② 화
2	① 바	② 봐	6	① 포	② 보
3	① 트	② 티	7	① 호	② 포
4	① 려	② 료	8	① 키	② 기

☐ CA-2. Listen and Write

Listen to the sound in **Lesson C > Listening Quiz 2** and write down the hangul sounds you hear in the exact order that you hear them in.

1	2	3	4	5	6	7	8	9	10

☐ CA-3. Listen and Number

Listen to the eight words in the sound file in **Lesson C > Listening Quiz 3**, then on the line below, number each word 1-8 underneath in the order that the words are spoken.

히터	도쿄	피자	키스
과자	티프	셔츠	스키

C | Lesson Answer Key

❑ Hangul Matching (answers)

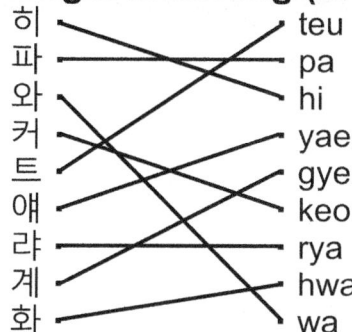

❑ CA-1. Listen and Choose (answers)

1	② 교	5	② 화
2	② 봐	6	① 포
3	① 트	7	① 호
4	② 료	8	② 기

❑ CA-2. Listen and Write (answers)

1	2	3	4	5	6	7	8	9	10
코	파	혀	표	져	과	샤	겨	애	트

❑ CA-3. Listen and Number (answers)

히터	도쿄	피자	키스
1	3	6	5
과자	티프	셔츠	스키
4	7	8	2

C | Hangul Practice Boxes

Use these boxes to practice writing the hangul you learned in lesson C.

Hangul From Zero! – Lesson D – Double Consonants 45

D | Korean Reading and Writing: Double Consonants

D | New Hangul

In this lesson we learn the final five consonants and six more vowels.

Consonants

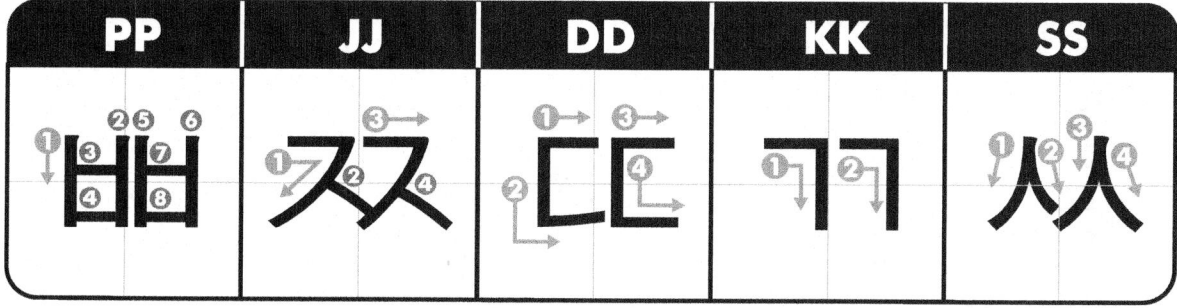

Practice writing by first tracing the gray, then writing on your own.

ㅃ	ㅃ	ㅃ					
ㅉ	ㅉ	ㅉ					
ㄸ	ㄸ	ㄸ					
ㄲ	ㄲ	ㄲ					
ㅆ	ㅆ	ㅆ					

Vowels

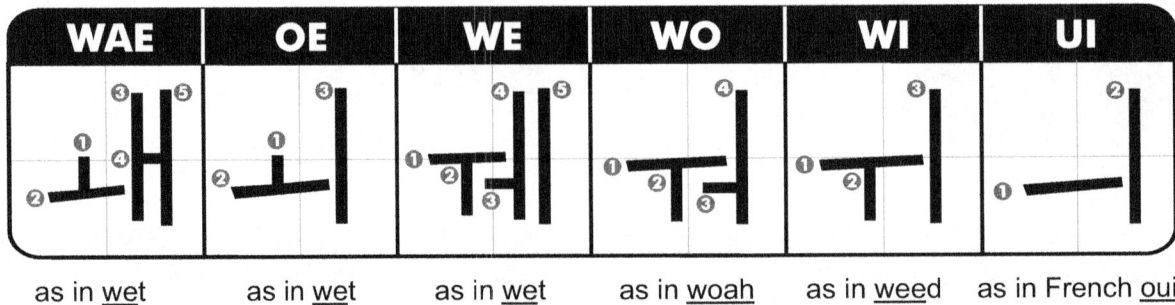

Practice writing by first tracing the gray, then writing on your own.

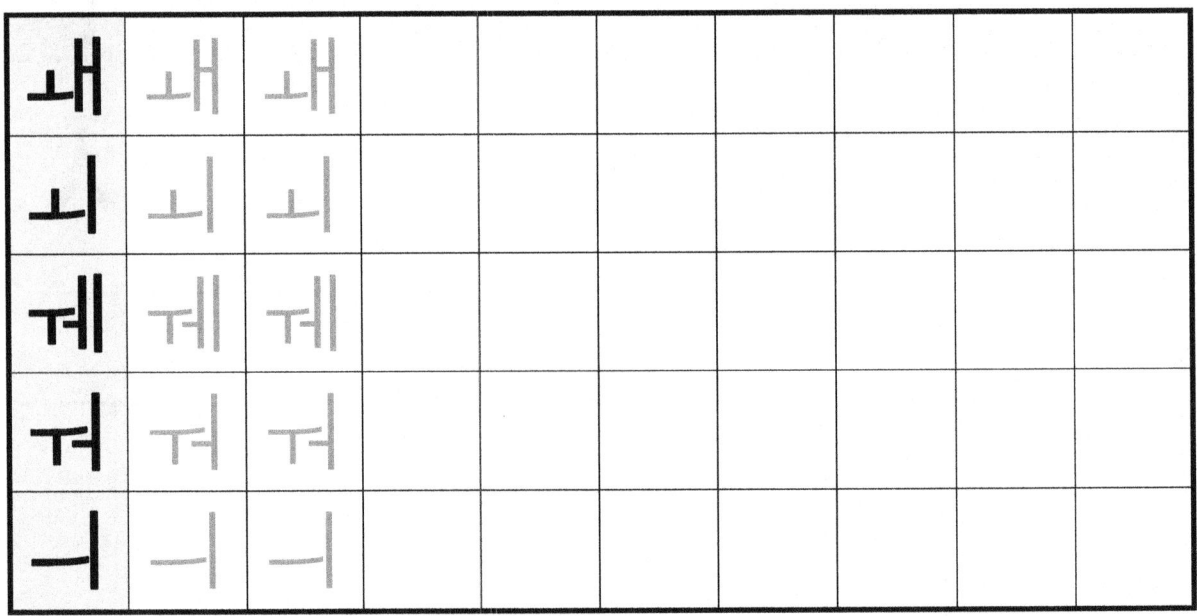

D | Hangul Facts

Now you have learned all of the current existing hangul used everyday in Korea. But… did you know there used to be other shapes including a triangle, dots, and even an X?

Currently there are 24 hangul letters containing 14 consonants and 10 vowels. However, in the original phonetic system initially created by King Sejong the Great there were 28 letters (or "Jamo" as they are called). The additional 4 Jamo eventually became obsolete.

D | Hangul Usage

❑ D-1. Double vowels
Double vowels are made by writing, or typing two of the vowels you have already learned together. They are written and input from the left vowel to right. Just like the single vowels, when they are used alone they still require the "null" character.

왜 (wae)   외 (oe)   워 (wo)   의 (ui)

❑ D-2. 위 vs 외 sound differences
These two double vowel types are commonly used in Korean. Despite looking similar in style, 외 is pronounced like the English word "WAY" and 위 is pronounced like the English word "WE". Perhaps this guy below will help you remember which is which.

❑ D-3. The double vowels
왜 ,외, and 웨, despite having different parts, all sound like the "WE" in "wet". When said slowly by your Korean friends, they might sound out the first part of the double vowel, but in spoken Korean you might not hear the sound difference. Listen to the words and see if you can see the difference in the "WE" sound.

왜	why?
외모	appearance
웨이터	waiter

❏ D-4. ㅟ and ㅢ sound differences

ㅟ and ㅢ might be tricky to pronounce since they are so close in sound. The sound change of these characters is similar to the sound change for ㅜ and ㅡ. For each sound, start with the "oo" part of "moon", then transition into the "ee" (like cl<u>ea</u>n). The only difference is the shape of your mouth when you say the "oo" part.

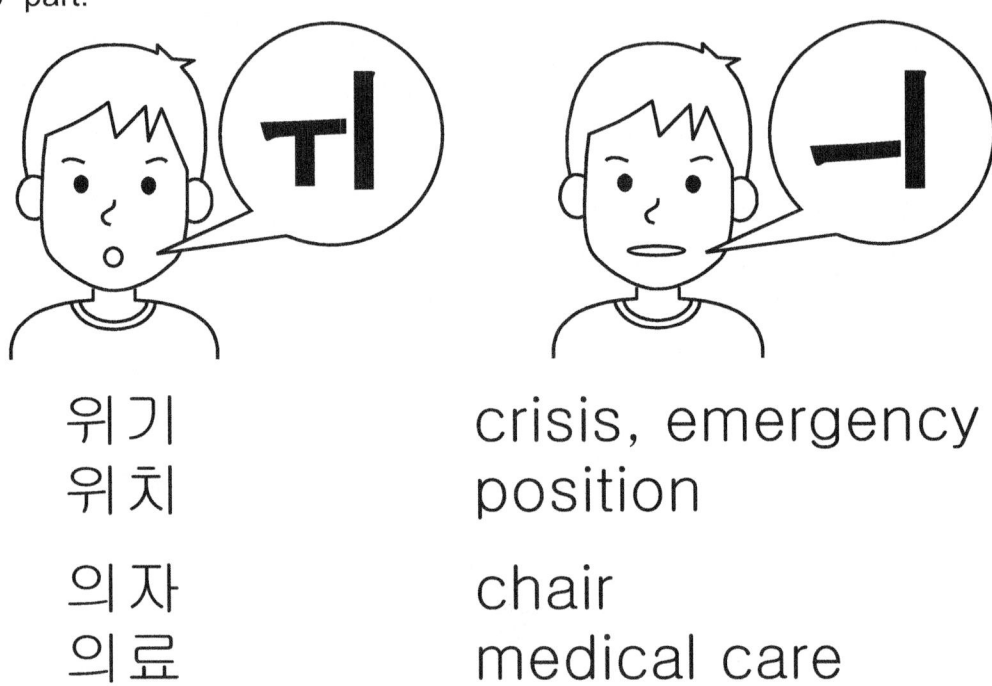

위기	crisis, emergency
위치	position
의자	chair
의료	medical care

❏ D-5. Double consonant sounds versus other sounds

ㅂ (b / p), ㅈ (j / ch), ㄷ (d / t), ㄱ (g / k) have a "hard" and "soft" sound. The double consonants ㅃ, ㅉ, ㄸ, ㄲ, and ㅆ are sounded out with more energy than single consonants. You push air into your mouth that is held back. You PAUSE slightly to let the pressure build. Then you release to make the sound. Try not to spit on anyone.

아빠	dad
가짜	fake
따로따로	separately
까치	magpie bird
싸개	wrapper, cover

D Writing Practice

First trace the light gray characters, then write each character 10 times.

sshi	씨										
we	웨										
ddo	또										
ggeu	끄										
ui	의										
jja	짜										
dwae	돼										
gwi	귀										
noe	뇌										
wo	워										
ppa	빠										
wi	위										

D | Words You Can Write

Using just the hangul from this lesson, we can already write many Korean words.

귀
ear

또
again

씨
family, clan (Mr., Mrs. etc)

뒤
back, rear

뇌
brain

뭐
what? huh?

짜다
salty

가위
scissors

외부
the outside

빼기
subtraction

꼬리
tail

의미
meaning

위치
position, location

궤도
orbit

돼지
pig

지뢰
land mine (explosive)

해외
overseas, abroad

가짜
fake

따로
separate

쓰레기
garbage, trash

D | Hangul Matching

Connect the dots between each hangul and the correct Romanization.

돼 ·		· sshi
짜 ·		· wi
빠 ·		· mwo
씨 ·		· dwae
꼬 ·		· dwi
위 ·		· ppa
뭐 ·		· jja
뒤 ·		· gwi
귀 ·		· kko

D | Listening Quiz

For this section you will need to listen to the audio provided for free at:
http://koreanfromzero.com/hangul/

❑ DA-1. Listen and Choose

Listen to the sounds in **Lesson D > Listening Quiz 1** then circle what you hear.

1	① 빠	② 파	5	① 의	② 위
2	① 치	② 찌	6	① 워	② 요
3	① 귀	② 궈	7	① 씨	② 띠
4	① 웨	② 페	8	① 되	② 대

Hangul From Zero! – Lesson D – Double Consonants

❑ DA-2. Listen and Write
Listen to the sound in **Lesson D > Listening Quiz 2** and write down the hangul sounds you hear in the exact order that you hear them in.

1	2	3	4	5	6	7	8	9	10

❑ DA-3. Listen and Number
Listen to the eight words in the sound file in **Lesson D > Listening Quiz 3**, then on the line below, number each word 1-8 underneath in the order that the words are spoken.

D Lesson Answer Key

❑ Hangul Matching (answers)

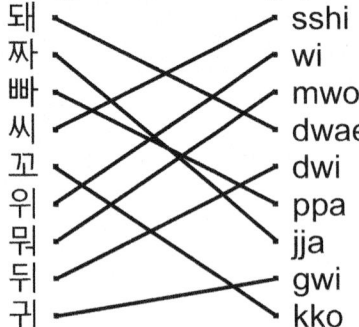

❑ DA-1. Listen and Choose (answers)

1	① 빠	5	② 위
2	② 찌	6	① 워
3	① 귀	7	② 띠
4	② 폐	8	② 대

❑ DA-2. Listen and Write (answers)

1	2	3	4	5	6	7	8	9	10
워	빠	씨	위	또	의	뇌	귀	짜	꾸

❑ DA-2. Listen and Number (answers)

돼지	가위	해외	꼬리
3	8	6	4
의사	가짜	빼기	따로
5	1	7	2

Hangul From Zero! – Lesson E – Final Consonants   55

Korean Reading and Writing: Final Consonants

There will be no new hangul vowels or consonants taught in this lesson, because you have learned all of them!

This lesson introduces the most important concept when learning hangul. Understanding the ideas taught in this lesson will allow you to conjugate verbs, adjectives and create even basic sentence structure.

E Hangul Usage

❑ E-1. Hangul with a "final consonant"
So far, all of the hangul characters in prior lessons have ended with a vowel and only had two parts. Now we will add consonants to the bottom of the character. These "final" consonants are called 받침 (batchim).

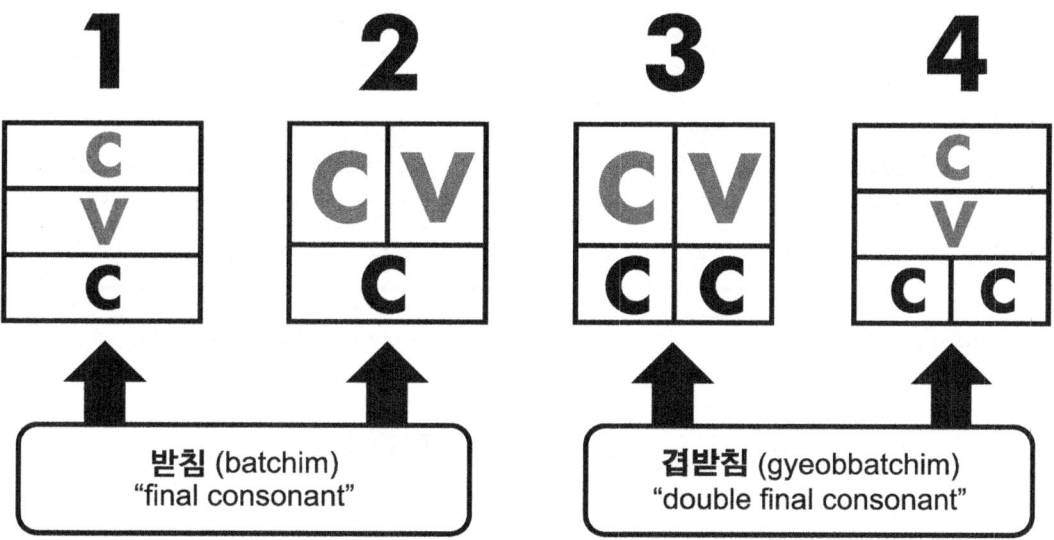

1 – A first consonant with a horizontal vowel and final consonant.
2 – A first consonant and a vertical vowel and final consonant.
3 – A first consonant with a vertical vowel and double final consonant.
4 – A first consonant with a horizontal vowel and double final consonant.

Now let's look at some actual complete hangul that have final consonants.

h	a	n	han
ㅎ +	ㅏ +	ㄴ =	한

g	eu	l	geul
ㄱ +	ㅡ +	ㄹ =	글

The following hangul characters are all built using the same initial consonant and vowel combination. The final consonant, 받침 (batchim), is the only thing that is different.

The black portion is the 받침 (batchim).

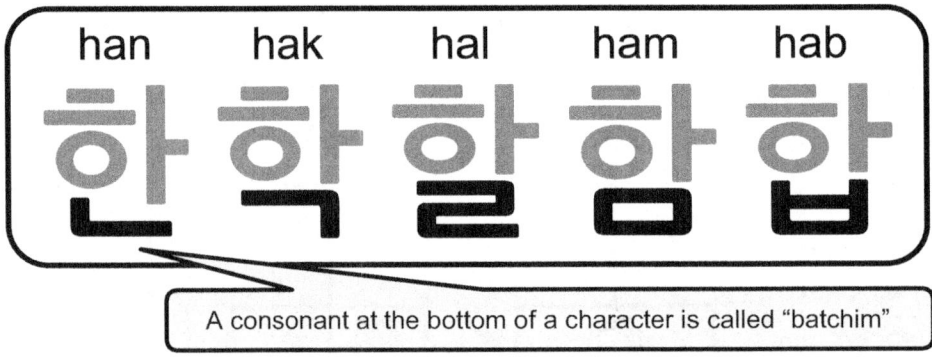

A consonant at the bottom of a character is called "batchim"

Here are some words that contain hangul with a final consonant.

한국	Korea
책	book
눈	eye, snow
손	hand
지갑	wallet

택시	taxi
감자	potato
발	foot
남자	man
친구	friend
사람	person
돈	money

❑ E-2. Answers to common questions

1. A vowel is never called batchim. There is no batchim if the character ends with a vowel.

2. ㅃ ㅉ ㄸ ㄲ ㅆ can be in the final position as a final consonant, but they aren't considered "double final consonants". They are just normal 받침.

Here are some example words that have 겹받침 (double batchim).

많다	to be many
닭갈비	chicken ribs
넓다	to be wide
읽다	to read
없다	to not have, not be

Here are some example words that have ㅃ, ㅆ, ㄲ, as 받침.
NOTE: ㅃ, ㅉ, ㄸ can't be in the final position. You can't even type it if you try.

있다	to have, be
닦다	to wipe, brush
맛있다	to be tasty
낚다	to hook, catch

❑ E-3. Double vowels
Some words have "double vowels".

사과	apple
귀	ear
의미	meaning
위치	position

❑ E-4. The "ng" sound when ㅇ is the final consonant
When ㅇ is used as the final consonant, then it is no longer silent and instead makes an "ng" sound.

```
g        a         ng        gang
ㄱ   +   ㅏ   +   ㅇ   =   강
```

```
j        eo        ng        jeong
ㅈ   +   ㅓ   +   ㅇ   =   정
```

The following words will contain a standalone vowel and / or a sound with ㅇ as the batchim.

안녕	goodbye
아이	child
이야기	a story

이유	reason
우산	umbrella
등	etc
방	room
요가	yoga
농담	a joke
오염	pollution
동물	animal
공항	airport

Ready for more fun? Here are words that have 2 ㅇ in some of their characters. The first ㅇ allows the vowel to stand alone without a consonant, and the second ㅇ is the "ng" sound as the batchim.

응급	emergency
고양이	cat
영국	United Kingdom
엉덩이	buttocks
양말	socks
옹알이	babbling
용	dragon
앵두	cherry

E | Hangul Matching

Connect the dots between each hangul and the correct Romanization.

한 · · nong
순 · · sun
냐 · · ggab
람 · · nyang
깝 · · ddeok
말 · · yong
용 · · han
농 · · mal
떡 · · ram

E | Listening Quiz

For this section you will need to listen to the audio provided for free at:
http://koreanfromzero.com/hangul/

❑ EA-1. Listen and Choose

Listen to the sounds in **Lesson E > Listening Quiz 1** then circle what you hear.

1	① 운	② 울	5	① 정	② 장
2	① 등	② 동	6	① 남	② 놈
3	① 감	② 갑	7	① 밥	② 밤
4	① 말	② 람	8	① 갈	② 골

❑ EA-2. Listen and Write

Listen to the sound in **Lesson E > Listening Quiz 2** and write down the hangul sounds you hear in the exact order that you hear them in.

1	2	3	4	5	6	7	8	9	10

❑ EA-3. Listen and Number

Listen to the eight words in the sound file in **Lesson E > Listening Quiz 3**, then on the line below, number each word 1-8 underneath in the order that the words are spoken.

E. Lesson Answer Key

❏ Hangul Matching (answers)

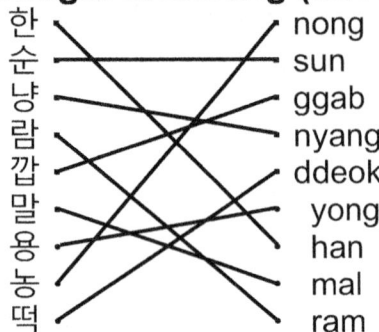

❏ EA-1. Listen and Choose (answers)

1	① 운	5	② 장
2	① 등	6	① 남
3	② 갑	7	① 밥
4	① 말	8	② 골

❏ EA-2. Listen and Write (answers)

1	2	3	4	5	6	7	8	9	10
강	글	책	눈	양	물	신	람	든	식

❏ EA-3. Listen and Number (answers)

앵두	양말	사과	택시
7	4	6	8
남자	동물	공항	우산
2	3	5	1

E | Hangul Practice Boxes

Use these boxes to practice writing the hangul you learned in lesson E.

Korean Reading and Writing: Sound Change Rules

Why is this lesson important?
When certain hangul are combined, their sounds can change in unexpected ways. You will eventually learn some words with spellings that don't match their pronunciation.

Check this lesson later!
As you learn more Korean, this lesson should be reviewed to make sure you aren't missing any common sound change rules.

F | Hangul Usage

❏ F-1. T-stops
When certain characters are used as a 받침 they are converted to "T" sound. We call this T sound a "T-stop". ㅅ, ㅈ, ㅊ, ㅎ are all T-stop characters. ㄷ and ㅌ are also T sound but since they are always a T sound, they are left out of the examples.

Example with T-stops
1. 이것 (pronounced 이걷) — this one
2. 늦게 (pronounced 늗게) — late
3. 몇 개 (pronounced 멷개) — how many?
4. 좋다 (pronounced 조타) — to be good (see section G-9)

When any T-stop consonant is followed by ㅇ(이응) then the T-stop is cancelled and the original sound returns.

"T" stop cancels when followed by 이응

겄이 받아 늦어 꽃이
geoshi bada neujeo ggochi

❏ F-2. "S" to "SH" sound with ㅅ

When ㅅ is combined with ㅣ, ㅕ, ㅑ, ㅛ, ㅠ the "S" changes to an "SH" sound. The sound REMAINS as "S" when combined with ㅏ, ㅓ, ㅜ, ㅗ, ㅡ, ㅐ, ㅔ.

Example of S and SH sound for ㅅ
1. 소시지 — sausage
2. 셔츠 — shirt
3. 쇼핑 — shopping
4. 샴푸 — shampoo
5. 슈퍼마켓 — super market
6. 사서 — librarian

❑ F-3. ㅅ followed by ㅎ

When ㅅ is followed by a ㅎ in the next hangul character the sound moves into the ㅎ position and is pronounced as ㅌ.

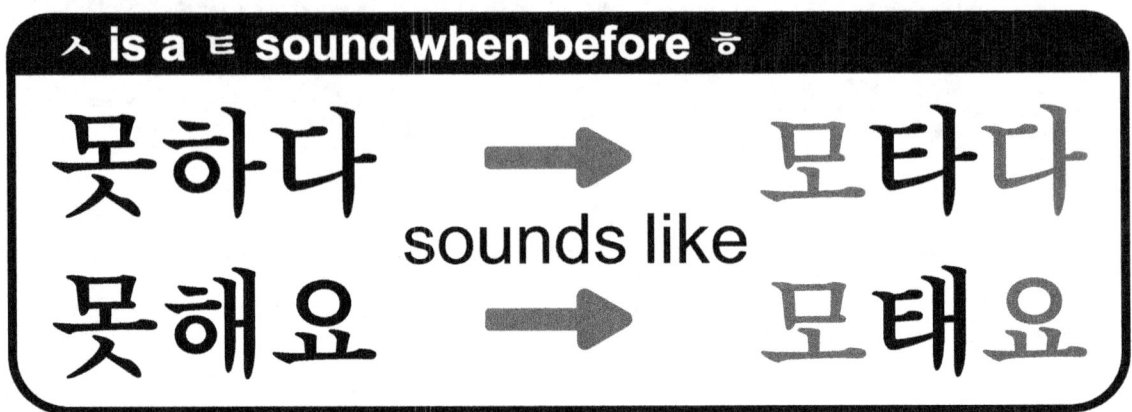

❑ F-4. "L" and "R" sound for ㄹ (리을)

When there are two ㄹ back to back the sound is always "L". When ㄹ is at the end of a word it's always an "L" sound. When ㄹ is at the beginning of a word it's an "R" sound.

F-5. ㄹ(리을) and ㄴ (니은) combinations

When a ㄹ is followed by a ㄴ OR the ㄴ is followed by ㄹ the combined sound changes to a double "L" sound.

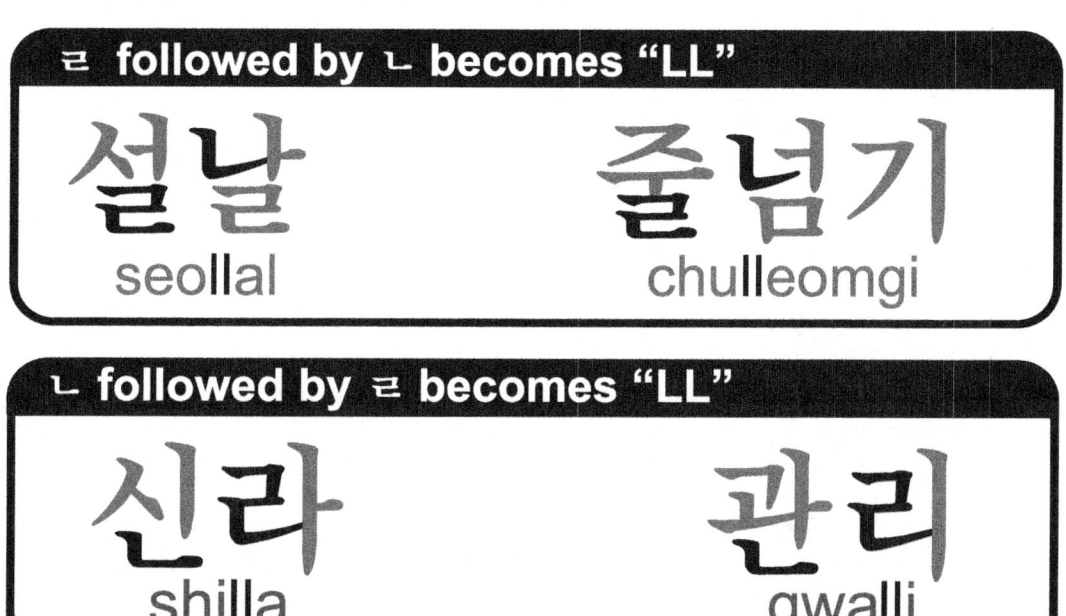

F-6. Silent 겹받침 (double consonant)

As discussed in a prior lesson, sometimes one of the double consonants in a double consonant is silent.

The double consonants you might see are ㄹㄱ, ㄹㅁ, ㄹㅍ, ㄹㅎ, and ㅂㅅ.

❑ F-7. The various sounds for 하다

Eventually you will learn about 하다 verbs, and this sound change will be important then. 하다 tends to blend into the hangul character before it.

1. Soft 하다

After you begin learning the 하다 verbs you might feel that it's RARE to hear 하다 actually as HADA. It often sounds like 아다 instead of 하다, or the H sound is weak.

Examples
1. 공부**하다** (sounds like 공부**아다**)   to study
2. 말**하다** (sounds like 마**라다**)   to tell, to talk
3. 단순**하다** (pronounced 단수**나다**)   to be simple

2. Harder sound before 하다

When consonants like ㄱ, ㅂ are followed by 하다 they blend into a harder sound. See section G-9 also.

Examples
1. 대답하다 (sounds like 대다**파다**)   to reply, to answer
2. 착하다 (sounds like 차**카다**)   to be kind

Special Information 특별 정보

SUMMARY: Learning VS actual speaking is different.
When you are learning Korean, and you have a friend or teacher helping you they might actually say the 하다 of 공부하다 etc as "HADA" because they are saying it slow.

The 하다 sound change is also common with other words that start with ㅎ.

Examples
1. 천천**히** (sounds like 천천**이**)   slowly
2. 안녕**하**세요 (sounds like 안녕**아**세요)   hello

F-8. Random CH sound when not expected (ㅌ and ㄷ)

When ㄷ is followed by ㅎ the resulting sound is "CH".
Similarly when ㅌ is followed by 이 the ㅌ changes to a "CH" sound.

> **Example CH sounds**
> 1. 끝이 (pronounced 끄치)   tip, end
> 2. 같이 (pronounced 가치)   together
> 3. 닫히다 (pronounced 다치다)   to shut

F-9. Shift to hard sound after and before ㅎ

When ㄱ, ㄷ, ㅂ, or ㅈ are before or after ㅎ their sound shifts to their harder sound counterparts ㅋ, ㅌ, ㅍ, and ㅊ.

Harder sound after ㅎ	
written as	sounds like
싫다 →	실타
좋지 →	조치
그렇게 →	그러케

Harder sound prior to ㅎ	
written as	sounds like
축하 →	추카
대답해 →	대다패

F | Hangul Practice Boxes

Use these boxes to practice writing the hangul you learned in lessons A-G.

 Korean Reading and Writing: Typing Hangul

In your life, you will probably type Korean a lot more than you will write it. Of course, when you are learning Korean, you will write it a lot, but when you are talking to your friends using chat programs on your phone or computer, you will be typing.

In order to type Korean on your computer you will need to first make sure you have installed the proper programs. You can go here for a tutorial on how to install Korean on your device.

http://www.KoreanFromZero.com/install-korean
(it's 100% free)

You can also purchase stickers for just a few dollars to place hangul on your own keyboard. Search Amazon.com or your favorite online store to see what is available.

G | Hangul Typing Points

❏ G-1. Typing your first and second characters

The Korean keyboard is designed to make it easy to type Korean. All the consonants (black) are on the left, and all the vowels (white) on are the right.

In order to make one character, we need at least two keystrokes. Even the most basic and the most complicated Korean character will start with a consonant (black key) followed by a vowel (white key). You can cut out the keyboard in the back of the book for easy reference.

As you type, the character will "build" on the screen. It might be confusing at first, but just keep typing. You do not have to "finish" a character. The keyboard input software knows when to end your character as long as you have correctly typed it.

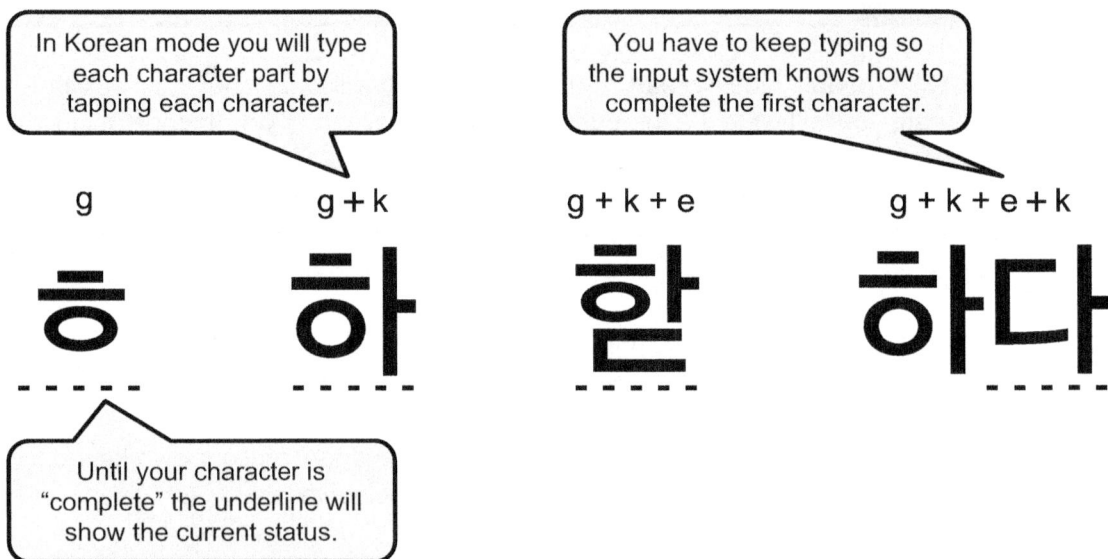

As you are typing, sometimes the 3rd key stroke gets added to the bottom of the first character, EVEN though you want this to be the 1st stroke of the 2nd character. DO NOT PANIC! Once you type the next vowel the 2nd character will be created. This is because NO Korean character can have a CVCV combination. Once the software sees CVCV it knows to make two characters. If it doesn't type what you want it to… YOU have made a mistake. You can always use backspace to erase just the last input.

❑ G-2. Shift characters

The "double consonants" require the shift key to be pressed first. Or, in the case of "double vowels", two vowels in a row will be required to complete the vowel.

Double Key Examples
shift + ㄷ = ㄸ
shift + ㅈ = ㅉ
ㅗ + ㅏ = ㅘ
ㅜ + ㅓ = ㅝ

Example Word
또 (again, once more)
짜다 (salty)
화요일 (Tuesday)
월요일 (Monday)

❑ G-3. Shortcuts and the spacebar (Windows)

On a Windows PC, you can cycle installed language input methods by pressing "ALT" key and ~ (top left key) at the same time. When in Korean mode, you can toggle to English input by hitting the RIGHT "ALT" key. The left one does NOT toggle. When you hit the space bar, the character you are working on will immediately complete and a space will be added.

❑ G-4. Hangul typing exercise

If you don't have stickers or a Korean keyboard, you can print a copy of the keyboard from the back of this book.

Now you should practice typing Korean. Here are some practice words along with the actual keys pressed to make them display. As you type each key, watch how the characters build on the screen.

The letters on top of each example are what you ACTUALLY type on your keyboard when you are in Korean mode.

rla cl

김치

Kimchee

gks rnr tk fka

한국사람

Korean person

dks sud gk tp dy
안녕하세요
Good Afternoon / Hello

dl rjt dms shift+wk dy
이것은 짜요
This is salty.

dh smf dms cn dnj dy
오늘은 추워요
Today is cold.

rhos cksg dk dy
괜찮아요
It's okay.

| wo | al | dl shift+t | dj | dy |

재미있어요

It's interesting.

| so | dlf | rkf | rj | d shift+p | dy |

내일 갈 거예요

I will go tomorrow.

250 Korean Vocabulary Words in Hangul

This word list was created to help you practice your new ability to read Hangul. Learning the words will start you on your next step of learning to speak Korean.

Each word group has 4 sections.

- **Reference List**
  This is a list of all the words to give you an easy way to reference each word.

- **Activities**
  These are activities to test your memory of the meaning of each word, and also to test you on the proper spelling in hangul.

- **Answer Key**
  This one is simply to check your answers. The answer key is always immediately following the activities area.

- **Front & Back Cards**
  This is to help you memorize the words and their meaning.

Hangul From Zero RESOURCES!

- Don't forget you can listen to ALL THE WORDS at
  http://koreanfromzero.com/hangul
  All vocab group sounds are available there!

Vocabulary Section 1: Body Words

1. 눈	eyes, snow
2. 코	nose
3. 입	mouth
4. 귀	ears
5. 손	hands
6. 발	feet
7. 손가락	finger
8. 어깨	shoulder
9. 무릎	knee
10. 팔꿈치	elbow
11. 발뒤꿈치	heel
12. 턱	chin
13. 배	stomach
14. 등	back
15. 목	neck, throat
16. 목구멍	throat
17. 이마	forehead
18. 손목	wrist
19. 입술	lips
20. 엉덩이	hip, butt

21. 가슴	chest, breast
22. 폐	lung
23. 위	stomach
24. 심장	heart
25. 근육	muscle
26. 뇌	brain
27. 피	blood
28. 몸	body
29. 손톱	finger nails
30. 발톱	toe nails

1 Vocabulary Activities

■ Word Match
Write the letter in the box next to the Korean word for the matching English.

A. eyes, snow	G. muscle
B. finger nails	H. hands
C. ears	I. shoulder
D. heart	J. heel
E. stomach	K. knee
F. chest, breast	L. neck, throat

☐ 손톱　　☐ 가슴　　☐ 발뒤꿈치
☐ 눈　　　☐ 귀　　　☐ 배
☐ 근육　　☐ 무릎　　☐ 심장
☐ 손　　　☐ 어깨　　☐ 목

■ Correct Korean
Choose the correct Korean for the English.

1. nose
　A. 코　　　B. 고　　　C. 콜　　　D. 쿠

2. lung
　A. 페　　　B. 베　　　C. 벡　　　D. 패

3. chin
　A. 덕　　　B. 턱　　　C. 덖　　　D. 탁

4. forehead
　A. 이머　　B. 일마　　C. 이마　　D. 이알

5. finger
　A. 손가닥　B. 손가락　C. 손가랅　D. 순가락

1 Answer Key

■ Word Match (answers)

A. eyes, snow
B. finger nails
C. ears
D. heart
E. stomach
F. chest, breast
G. muscle
H. hands
I. shoulder
J. heel
K. knee
L. neck, throat

[B] 손톱
[A] 눈
[G] 근육
[H] 손
[F] 가슴
[C] 귀
[K] 무릎
[I] 어깨
[J] 발뒤꿈치
[E] 배
[D] 심장
[L] 목

■ Correct Korean (answers)

1. nose
   A. 코   B. 고   C. 콭   D. 쿠
2. lung
   A. 폐   B. 베   C. 벡   D. 패
3. chin
   A. 덕   **B. 턱**   C. 덖   D. 탁
4. forehead
   A. 이머   B. 잍마   **C. 이마**   D. 이알
5. finger
   A. 손가닥   **B. 손가락**   C. 손가랔   D. 순가락

2 코	1 눈
4 귀	3 입
6 발	5 손
8 어깨	7 손가락
10 팔꿈치	9 무릎

1 eyes, snow	**2** nose
3 mouth	**4** ears
5 hands	**6** feet
7 finger	**8** shoulder
9 knee	**10** elbow

12 턱	11 발뒤꿈치
14 등	13 배
16 목구멍	15 목
18 손목	17 이마
20 엉덩이	19 입술

11 **heel**	12 **chin**
13 **stomach**	14 **back**
15 **neck, throat**	16 **throat**
17 **forehead**	18 **wrist**
19 **lips**	20 **hip, butt**

22 폐	21 가슴
24 심장	23 위
26 뇌	25 근육
28 몸	27 피
30 발톱	29 손톱

21	22
chest, breast	lung

23	24
stomach	heart

25	26
muscle	brain

27	28
blood	body

29	30
finger nails	toe nails

Vocabulary Section 2: Famous Products

31. 아이폰	iPhone ®
32. 갤럭시	Galaxy ® (Samsung)
33. 안도로이드	Android ®
34. 애플	Apple ®
35. 윈도우	Windows ®
36. 맥도날드	McDonald's ®
37. 스타벅스	Starbucks ®
38. 구글	Google ®
39. 네이버	Naver ®
40. 삼성	Samsung ®
41. 현대	Hyundai ®
42. 아이패드	iPad ®
43. 코카콜라	Coca Cola ®
44. 페이스북	Facebook ®
45. 디즈니	Disney ®
46. 토요타	Toyota ®
47. 틱톡	TikTok ®
48. 소니	Sony ®
49. 대한항공	Korean Air ®
50. 유튜브	YouTube

2 Vocabulary Activities

■ Word Match
Write the letter in the box next to the Korean word for the matching English.

A. TikTok ®
B. Windows ®
C. iPhone ®
D. Naver ®
E. Galaxy ® (Samsung)
F. Facebook ®
G. McDonald's ®
H. Samsung ®
I. Sony ®
J. Coca Cola ®
K. Apple ®
L. Google ®

☐ 갤럭시   ☐ 윈도우   ☐ 페이스북
☐ 코카콜라   ☐ 아이폰   ☐ 맥도날드
☐ 애플   ☐ 틱톡   ☐ 네이버
☐ 삼성   ☐ 소니   ☐ 구글

■ Correct Korean
Choose the correct Korean for the English.

1. Toyota ®
A. 토요타   B. 토요텁   C. 토못타   D. 토요터

2. iPad ®
A. 아이패둣 B. 아이패튼 C. 아민패드 D. 아이패드

3. Disney ®
A. 디즈니   B. 둫즈니   C. 드즈니   D. 디줄니

4. Android ®
A. 안도로이드 B. 언도로이드 C. 업도로이드 D. 안도로으드

5. Korean Air ®
A. 대헌항공 B. 댈한항공 C. 대한앙공 D. 대한항공

2 Answer Key

■ Word Match (answers)

A. TikTok ®
B. Windows ®
C. iPhone ®
D. Naver ®
E. Galaxy ® (Samsung)
F. Facebook ®
G. McDonald's ®
H. Samsung ®
I. Sony ®
J. Coca Cola ®
K. Apple ®
L. Google ®

[E] 갤럭시 [B] 윈도우 [F] 페이스북
[J] 코카콜라 [C] 아이폰 [G] 맥도날드
[K] 애플 [A] 틱톡 [D] 네이버
[H] 삼성 [I] 소니 [L] 구글

■ Correct Korean (answers)

1. Toyota ®
- **A. 토요타**
- B. 토요텁
- C. 토못타
- D. 토요터

2. iPad ®
- A. 아이패둣
- B. 아이패튼
- C. 아민패드
- **D. 아이패드**

3. Disney ®
- **A. 디즈니**
- B. 둫즈니
- C. 드즈니
- D. 디줄니

4. Android ®
- **A. 안도로이드**
- B. 언도로이드
- C. 업도로이드
- D. 안도로으드

5. Korean Air ®
- A. 대헌항공
- B. 댈한항공
- C. 대한앙공
- **D. 대한항공**

2 Additional Writing Practice Area

32 갤럭시	31 아이폰
34 애플	33 안도로이드
36 맥도날드	35 윈도우
38 구글	37 스타벅스
40 삼성	39 네이버

31	32
iPhone ®	Galaxy ® (Samsung)

33	34
Android ®	Apple ®

35	36
Windows ®	McDonald's ®

37	38
Starbucks ®	Google ®

39	40
Naver ®	Samsung ®

41 현대	**42** 아이패드
43 코카콜라	**44** 페이스북
45 디즈니	**46** 토요타
47 틱톡	**48** 소니
49 대한항공	**50** 유튜브

41 Hyundai ®	42 iPad ®
43 Coca Cola ®	44 Facebook ®
45 Disney ®	46 Toyota ®
47 TikTok ®	48 Sony ®
49 Korean Air ®	50 YouTube

3 Vocabulary Section 3: Jobs

51.	판매원	salesperson
52.	파일럿	pilot
53.	사진 작가	photographer
54.	장관	minister
55.	편집자	editor
56.	작가	writer, author
57.	기술자	engineer
58.	디자이너	designer
59.	배우	actor, actress
60.	선생님	teacher
61.	신문기자	journalist
62.	건축가	architect
63.	수의사	veterinarian
64.	이발사	barber
65.	미용사	hairdresser
66.	회계사	accountant
67.	공무원	government worker
68.	회사원	an office worker
69.	소방관	firefighter
70.	과학자	scientist

71. 정치가	politician
72. 의사	doctor
73. 간호사	nurse
74. 인플루언서	influencer
75. 가수	singer
76. 요리사	chef
77. 연예인	celebrity
78. 사장님	boss, president (of company)
79. 우주 비행사	astronaut
80. 비서	secretary

Hangul From Zero! - 250 Words Section 3 - Jobs   **97**

3 Vocabulary Activities

■ Word Match

Write the letter in the box next to the Korean word for the matching English.

A. accountant	G. salesperson
B. actor, actress	H. chef
C. hairdresser	I. singer
D. influencer	J. photographer
E. architect	K. firefighter
F. celebrity	L. politician

☐ 회계사   ☐ 건축가   ☐ 배우
☐ 연예인   ☐ 사진 작가   ☐ 미용사
☐ 판매원   ☐ 소방관   ☐ 인플루언서
☐ 요리사   ☐ 가수   ☐ 정치가

■ Correct Korean

Choose the correct Korean for the English.

1. scientist
 A. 과악자   B. 과학자   C. 과핰자   D. 과학찿

2. astronaut
 A. 우주 비행사   B. 울주 비행사   C. 우주 빋행사   D. 우주 비행설

3. boss, president (of company)
 A. 자장님   B. 사장님   C. 사장늪   D. 사장늧

4. designer
 A. 디점이너   B. 디자이너   C. 디자이남   D. 디저이너

5. engineer
 A. 기줄자   B. 기술자   C. 기슢자   D. 기술저

3 Answer Key

■ Word Match (answers)

A. accountant
B. actor, actress
C. hairdresser
D. influencer
E. architect
F. celebrity
G. salesperson
H. chef
I. singer
J. photographer
K. firefighter
L. politician

[A] 회계사　　[E] 건축가　　[B] 배우
[F] 연예인　　[J] 사진 작가　[C] 미용사
[G] 판매원　　[K] 소방관　　[D] 인플루언서
[H] 요리사　　[I] 가수　　　[L] 정치가

■ Correct Korean (answers)

1. scientist
   A. 과악자　　**B. 과학자**　　C. 과핰자　　D. 과학챃
2. astronaut
   A. 우주 비행사　B. 울주 비행사　C. 우주 빈행사　D. 우주 비행설
3. boss, president (of company)
   A. 자장님　　**B. 사장님**　　C. 사장늪　　D. 사장늧
4. designer
   A. 디점이너　**B. 디자이너**　C. 디자이남　D. 디저이너
5. engineer
   A. 기줄자　　**B. 기술자**　　C. 기슿자　　D. 기술저

52 파일럿	51 판매원
54 장관	53 사진 작가
56 작가	55 편집자
58 디자이너	57 기술자
60 선생님	59 배우

51 salesperson	52 pilot
53 photographer	54 minister
55 editor	56 writer, author
57 engineer	58 designer
59 actor, actress	60 teacher

62 건축가	61 신문기자
64 이발사	63 수의사
66 회계사	65 미용사
68 회사원	67 공무원
70 과학자	69 소방관

61 journalist	62 architect
63 veterinarian	64 barber
65 hairdresser	66 accountant
67 government worker	68 an office worker
69 firefighter	70 scientist

72	71
의사	정치가

74	73
인플루언서	간호사

76	75
요리사	가수

78	77
사장님	연예인

80	79
비서	우주 비행사

71 politician	72 doctor
73 nurse	74 influencer
75 singer	76 chef
77 celebrity	78 boss, president (of company)
79 astronaut	80 secretary

4 Vocabulary Section 4: School Words

81. 학교	school
82. 유치원	kindergarten
83. 초등학교	elementary school
84. 중학교	middle school
85. 고등 학교	high school
86. 전문 대학	college
87. 4년제 대학	university
88. 체육실	gymnasium
89. 강당	auditorium
90. 매점	small shop
91. 교무실	teacher's office
92. 국어학	national language (Korean etc.)
93. 생물학	biology
94. 물리학	physics
95. 화학	chemistry
96. 수학	mathematics
97. 기하학	geometry
98. 역사학	history
99. 지리학	geography
100. 체육	physical education

101. 1학년	freshman
102. 2학년	sophomore
103. 3학년	junior
104. 4학년	senior
105. 학부생	undergraduate
106. 대학원생	graduate
107. 학사	bachelor
108. 석사	master
109. 수업료, 학비	tuition
110. 장학금	scholarship
111. 학기	semester, term, quarter
112. 성적 증명서	transcript
113. 졸업 증서	diploma
114. 교수님	professor
115. 학원	private academy
116. 점수	score; points (on test / in game)
117. 전공	major
118. 부전공	minor
119. 유학	studying abroad
120. 휴학	leave of absence from school

4 Vocabulary Activities

Word Match

Write the letter in the box next to the Korean word for the matching English.

A. bachelor
B. undergraduate
C. high school
D. national language (Korean etc.)
E. college
F. geography
G. geometry
H. graduate
I. semester, term, quarter
J. sophomore
K. teacher's office
L. chemistry

☐ 학부생   ☐ 지리학   ☐ 2학년
☐ 고등 학교 ☐ 기하학   ☐ 교무실
☐ 학사   ☐ 국어학   ☐ 대학원생
☐ 학기   ☐ 화학   ☐ 전문 대학

Correct Korean

Choose the correct Korean for the English.

1. freshman
   A. 1학겨   B. 간학년   C. 1학년   D. 값학년

2. gymnasium
   A. 체뮥실   B. 체육실   C. 체윰실   D. 체육슬

3. mathematics
   A. 수핚   B. 수학   C. 수앜   D. 수헉

4. physical education
   A. 체육   B. 채육   C. 체윸   D. 제육

5. senior
   A. 갈학년   B. 4학낟   C. 4학년   D. 4악년

4 Answer Key

■ Word Match (answers)

A. bachelor
B. undergraduate
C. high school
D. national language (Korean etc.)
E. college
F. geography
G. geometry
H. graduate
I. semester, term, quarter
J. sophomore
K. teacher's office
L. chemistry

[B] 학부생   [F] 지리학   [J] 2학년
[C] 고등 학교   [G] 기하학   [K] 교무실
[A] 학사   [D] 국어학   [H] 대학원생
[I] 학기   [L] 화학   [E] 전문 대학

■ Correct Korean (answers)

1. freshman
   A. 1학격   B. 간학년   **C. 1학년**   D. 갔학년
2. gymnasium
   A. 체뮥실   **B. 체육실**   C. 체윾실   D. 체육슬
3. mathematics
   A. 수핡   **B. 수학**   C. 수앞   D. 수헉
4. physical education
   A. 체육   B. 채육   C. 체윾   D. 제육
5. senior
   A. 갈학년   B. 4학낱   **C. 4학년**   D. 4악년

82 유치원	81 학교
84 중학교	83 초등학교
86 전문 대학	85 고등 학교
88 체육실	87 4년제 대학
90 매점	89 강당

81 school	82 kindergarten
83 elementary school	84 middle school
85 high school	86 college
87 university	88 gymnasium
89 auditorium	90 small shop

92	91
국어학	교무실

94	93
물리학	생물학

96	95
수학	화학

98	97
역사학	기하학

100	99
체육	지리학

91 teacher's office	92 national language (Korean etc.)
93 biology	94 physics
95 chemistry	96 mathematics
97 geometry	98 history
99 geography	100 physical education

102	101
2학년	1학년

104	103
4학년	3학년

106	105
대학원생	학부생

108	107
석사	학사

110	109
장학금	수업료, 학비

101	102
freshman	sophomore

103	104
junior	senior

105	106
undergraduate	graduate

107	108
bachelor	master

109	110
tuition	scholarship

112 성적 증명서	111 학기
114 교수님	113 졸업 증서
116 점수	115 학원
118 부전공	117 전공
120 휴학	119 유학

111	112
semester, term, quarter	transcript

113	114
diploma	professor

115	116
private academy	score; points (on test / in game)

117	118
major	minor

119	120
studying abroad	leave of absence from school

Vocabulary Section 5: Animals

#	Korean	English
121.	개구리	frog
122.	거북이	turtle
123.	악어	crocodile
124.	사슴	deer
125.	도마뱀	lizard
126.	참새	sparrow
127.	제비	swallow
128.	백조	swan
129.	다람쥐	squirrel
130.	학	crane
131.	사자	lion
132.	포유 동물	mammal
133.	올빼미	owl
134.	돌고래	dolphin
135.	고래	whale
136.	늑대	wolf
137.	소	cow
138.	앵무새	parrot
139.	여우	fox
140.	동물원	zoo

141. 개	dog
142. 고양이	cat
143. 쥐	mouse
144. 펭귄	penguin
145. 곰	bear
146. 하마	hippo
147. 기린	giraffe
148. 코끼리	elephant
149. 물고기	fish
150. 새	bird

5 Vocabulary Activities

Word Match
Write the letter in the box next to the Korean word for the matching English.

A. bear	G. turtle
B. elephant	H. dog
C. lizard	I. whale
D. bird	J. giraffe
E. crane	K. lion
F. deer	L. owl

☐ 코끼리　　☐ 사슴　　☐ 기린
☐ 곰　　　　☐ 도마뱀　☐ 학
☐ 거북이　　☐ 사자　　☐ 새
☐ 개　　　　☐ 고래　　☐ 올빼미

Correct Korean
Choose the correct Korean for the English.

1. mammal
   A. 포유 돔물   B. 포윹 동물   C. 포유 동욷   D. 포유 동물

2. dolphin
   A. 돌고대   B. 돌코래   C. 돋고래   D. 돌고래

3. fox
   A. 염우   B. 며우   C. 여우   D. 여뭊

4. frog
   A. 개귿리   B. 캐구리   C. 개구리   D. 개쿳리

5. hippo
   A. 학마   B. 하앟   C. 하마   D. 하압

5 Answer Key

■ Word Match (answers)

A. bear
B. elephant
C. lizard
D. bird
E. crane
F. deer
G. turtle
H. dog
I. whale
J. giraffe
K. lion
L. owl

[B] 코끼리　　[F] 사슴　　[J] 기린
[A] 곰　　　　[C] 도마뱀　[E] 학
[G] 거북이　　[K] 사자　　[D] 새
[H] 개　　　　[I] 고래　　[L] 올빼미

■ Correct Korean (answers)

1. mammal
 A. 포유 돔물　　B. 포윻 동물　　C. 포유 동울　　**D. 포유 동물**

2. dolphin
 A. 돌고대　　B. 돌코래　　C. 돋고래　　**D. 돌고래**

3. fox
 A. 염우　　B. 며우　　**C. 여우**　　D. 여뭋

4. frog
 A. 개귿리　　B. 캐구리　　**C. 개구리**　　D. 개쿳리

5. hippo
 A. 학마　　B. 하앟　　**C. 하마**　　D. 하압

122	121
거북이	개구리

124	123
사슴	악어

126	125
참새	도마뱀

128	127
백조	제비

130	129
학	다람쥐

121 frog	122 turtle
123 crocodile	124 deer
125 lizard	126 sparrow
127 swallow	128 swan
129 squirrel	130 crane

132 포유 동물	131 사자
134 돌고래	133 올빼미
136 늑대	135 고래
138 앵무새	137 소
140 동물원	139 여우

131	132
lion	mammal

133	134
owl	dolphin

135	136
whale	wolf

137	138
cow	parrot

139	140
fox	zoo

142 고양이	141 개
144 펭귄	143 쥐
146 하마	145 곰
148 코끼리	147 기린
150 새	149 물고기

141 dog	142 cat
143 mouse	144 penguin
145 bear	146 hippo
147 giraffe	148 elephant
149 fish	150 bird

Vocabulary Section 6: Nature Words

#	Korean	English
151.	번개	lightning
152.	천둥	thunder
153.	구름	clouds
154.	개울	stream, brook
155.	일몰	sunset
156.	일출	sunrise
157.	절벽	cliff
158.	언덕	hill
159.	분수	fountain
160.	홍수	flood
161.	태풍	typhoon
162.	폭포	waterfall
163.	지진	earthquake
164.	경치	scenery
165.	수평선	horizon
166.	지구	Earth (the planet)
167.	대륙	continent
168.	해양	ocean
169.	바다	sea, ocean
170.	적도	equator

171. 남극	south pole
172. 북극	north pole
173. 강	river
174. 호수	lake
175. 산	mountain
176. 숲	forest
177. 봄	spring
178. 여름	summer
179. 가을	autumn
180. 겨울	winter

6 Vocabulary Activities

■ Word Match
Write the letter in the box next to the Korean word for the matching English.

A. south pole	G. sea, ocean
B. lake	H. sunrise
C. waterfall	I. hill
D. flood	J. river
E. Earth (the planet)	K. cliff
F. north pole	L. clouds

☐ 호수   ☐ 북극   ☐ 강
☐ 폭포   ☐ 바다   ☐ 절벽
☐ 남극   ☐ 홍수   ☐ 지구
☐ 일출   ☐ 언덕   ☐ 구름

■ Correct Korean
Choose the correct Korean for the English.

1. summer
  A. 몌름   B. 얏름   C. 여름   D. 야름

2. continent
  A. 대륙   B. 대륰   C. 뎈륙   D. 댄륙

3. lightning
  A. 번개   B. 번캐   C. 벅개   D. 펀개

4. ocean
  A. 앵양   B. 해영   C. 해먕   D. 해양

5. horizon
  A. 줄평선   B. 수병선   C. 수평선   D. 수팔선

6 Answer Key

Word Match (answers)

A. south pole
B. lake
C. waterfall
D. flood
E. Earth (the planet)
F. north pole
G. sea, ocean
H. sunrise
I. hill
J. river
K. cliff
L. clouds

[B] 호수   [F] 북극   [J] 강
[C] 폭포   [G] 바다   [K] 절벽
[A] 남극   [D] 홍수   [E] 지구
[H] 일출   [I] 언덕   [L] 구름

Correct Korean (answers)

1. summer
   A. 몉름   B. 얏름   **C. 여름**   D. 야름
2. continent
   A. 대륙   B. 대륚   C. 뎈륙   D. 댄륙
3. lightning
   A. 번개   B. 번캐   C. 벅개   D. 펀개
4. ocean
   A. 앵양   B. 해영   C. 해먕   **D. 해양**
5. horizon
   A. 줄평선   B. 수병선   **C. 수평선**   D. 수팔선

152 천둥	151 번개
154 개울	153 구름
156 일출	155 일몰
158 언덕	157 절벽
160 홍수	159 분수

151	152
lightning	thunder

153	154
clouds	stream, brook

155	156
sunset	sunrise

157	158
cliff	hill

159	160
fountain	flood

162 폭포	161 태풍
164 경치	163 지진
166 지구	165 수평선
168 해양	167 대륙
170 적도	169 바다

161 typhoon	**162** waterfall
163 earthquake	**164** scenery
165 horizon	**166** Earth (the planet)
167 continent	**168** ocean
169 sea, ocean	**170** equator

172 북극	171 남극
174 호수	173 강
176 숲	175 산
178 여름	177 봄
180 겨울	179 가을

171	172
south pole	north pole

173	174
river	lake

175	176
mountain	forest

177	178
spring	summer

179	180
autumn	winter

Vocabulary Section 7: Restaurant Words

#	Korean	English
181.	그릇	bowl
182.	접시	plate
183.	젓가락	chopsticks
184.	숟가락	spoon
185.	칼	knife
186.	포크	fork
187.	컵	cup
188.	반찬	side dish
189.	영수증	receipt
190.	따로따로	separately
191.	계산서	check, bill
192.	메뉴	menu
193.	주문	order
194.	휴지	napkin
195.	빨대	straw
196.	이쑤시개	toothpick
197.	디저트	dessert
198.	식당	restaurant
199.	종업원	waiter, waitress, food server
200.	가격	price

7 Vocabulary Activities

Word Match

Write the letter in the box next to the Korean word for the matching English.

A. waiter, waitress, food server	G. check, bill
B. dessert	H. chopsticks
C. menu	I. price
D. order	J. receipt
E. plate	K. side dish
F. knife	L. toothpick

☐ 종업원 ☐ 디저트 ☐ 칼
☐ 영수증 ☐ 메뉴   ☐ 계산서
☐ 반찬   ☐ 주문   ☐ 접시
☐ 젓가락 ☐ 가격   ☐ 이쑤시개

Correct Korean

Choose the correct Korean for the English.

1. fork
   A. 포큼   B. 포크   C. 붛크   D. 볻크
2. napkin
   A. 휴즐   B. 후지   C. 휴지   D. 율지
3. spoon
   A. 슴가락 B. 숟가락 C. 숟가락 D. 숟거락
4. restaurant
   A. 식덜   B. 식당   C. 식탕   D. 식탐
5. straw
   A. 뻘대   B. 빤대   C. 빨탤   D. 빨대

Hangul From Zero! - 250 Words Section 7 - Restaurant Words

7 Answer Key

■ Word Match (answers)

A. waiter, waitress, food server
B. dessert
C. menu
D. order
E. plate
F. knife
G. check, bill
H. chopsticks
I. price
J. receipt
K. side dish
L. toothpick

[A] 종업원   [B] 디저트   [F] 칼
[J] 영수증   [C] 메뉴   [G] 계산서
[K] 반찬   [D] 주문   [E] 접시
[H] 젓가락   [I] 가격   [L] 이쑤시개

■ Correct Korean (answers)

1. fork
 A. 포큭   **B. 포크**   C. 봉크   D. 볻크

2. napkin
 A. 휴즐   B. 후지   **C. 휴지**   D. 욷지

3. spoon
 A. 슴가락   **B. 숟가락**   C. 숟가락   D. 숟거락

4. restaurant
 A. 식덜   **B. 식당**   C. 식탕   D. 식탐

5. straw
 A. 뻘대   B. 빧대   C. 빨탤   **D. 빨대**

7 Additional Writing Practice Area

181	182
그릇	접시

183	184
젓가락	숟가락

185	186
칼	포크

187	188
컵	반찬

189	190
영수증	따로따로

181	182
bowl	plate

183	184
chopsticks	spoon

185	186
knife	fork

187	188
cup	side dish

189	190
receipt	separately

192	191
메뉴	계산서

194	193
휴지	주문

196	195
이쑤시개	빨대

198	197
식당	디저트

200	199
가격	종업원

191 check, bill	192 menu
193 order	194 napkin
195 straw	196 toothpick
197 dessert	198 restaurant
199 waiter, waitress, food server	200 price

Vocabulary Section 8: Foods

201.	간식	snack
202.	과일	fruit
203.	야채	vegetable
204.	고기	meat
205.	귤	tangerine / mandarin orange
206.	오이	cucumber
207.	버섯	mushroom
208.	멜론	melon
209.	빵	bread
210.	계란	egg
211.	우유	milk
212.	사탕	candy
213.	떡	rice cakes
214.	음료수	beverage (non-alcoholic)
215.	라면	ramen noodles
216.	감자	potato
217.	감자튀김	French fries
218.	삼각김밥	triangle-shaped gimbap
219.	불고기	roast meat (fire meat)
220.	갈비	ribs

221. 닭갈비	chicken ribs
222. 치킨	chicken
223. 포도	grapes
224. 수박	watermelon
225. 배	pear
226. 치즈	cheese
227. 바나나	banana
228. 토마토	tomato
229. 상추	lettuce
230. 당근	carrot

8 Vocabulary Activities

Word Match

Write the letter in the box next to the Korean word for the matching English.

```
A. French fries                G. ramen noodles
B. beverage (non-alcoholic)    H. tomato
C. banana                      I. rice cakes
D. bread                       J. snack
E. pear                        K. cheese
F. potato                      L. meat
```

☐ 음료수   ☐ 감자   ☐ 간식
☐ 감자튀김   ☐ 바나나   ☐ 배
☐ 라면   ☐ 떡   ☐ 치즈
☐ 빵   ☐ 토마토   ☐ 고기

Correct Korean

Choose the correct Korean for the English.

1. vegetable
  A. 야채   B. 얖채   C. 먀채   D. 먖채

2. egg
  A. 계란   B. 곌란   C. 켸란   D. 걔란

3. milk
  A. 은유   B. 우읃   C. 우유   D. 우윤

4. ribs
  A. 갈비   B. 갈핑   C. 것비   D. 갈븥

5. melon
  A. 맬론   B. 먲론   C. 멜룬   D. 멜론

8 Answer Key

■ Word Match (answers)

A. French fries
B. beverage (non-alcoholic)
C. banana
D. bread
E. pear
F. potato
G. ramen noodles
H. tomato
I. rice cakes
J. snack
K. cheese
L. meat

[B] 음료수 [F] 감자 [J] 간식
[A] 감자튀김 [C] 바나나 [E] 배
[G] 라면 [I] 떡 [K] 치즈
[D] 빵 [H] 토마토 [L] 고기

■ Correct Korean (answers)

1. vegetable
   A. 야채   B. 얖채   C. 먀채   D. 먛채
2. egg
   A. 계란   B. 곌란   C. 케란   D. 개란
3. milk
   A. 은유   B. 우윺   **C. 우유**   D. 우윤
4. ribs
   A. 갈비   B. 갈핑   C. 것비   D. 갈븉
5. melon
   A. 맬론   B. 맢론   C. 멜룬   **D. 멜론**

202 과일	201 간식
204 고기	203 야채
206 오이	205 귤
208 멜론	207 버섯
210 계란	209 빵

201	202
snack	fruit

203	204
vegetable	meat

205	206
tangerine / mandarin orange	cucumber

207	208
mushroom	melon

209	210
bread	egg

212 사탕	211 우유
214 음료수	213 떡
216 감자	215 라면
218 삼각김밥	217 감자튀김
220 갈비	219 불고기

211	212
milk	candy

213	214
rice cakes	beverage (non-alcoholic)

215	216
ramen noodles	potato

217	218
French fries	triangle-shaped gimbap

219	220
roast meat (fire meat)	ribs

222	221
치킨	닭갈비

224	223
수박	포도

226	225
치즈	배

228	227
토마토	바나나

230	229
당근	상추

221	222
chicken ribs	chicken

223	224
grapes	watermelon

225	226
pear	cheese

227	228
banana	tomato

229	230
lettuce	carrot

Vocabulary Section 9: People etc.

231. 여자	girl, woman
232. 남자	boy, man
233. 여자친구	girlfriend
234. 남자친구	boyfriend
235. 부모님	parents
236. 할아버지	grandfather
237. 할머니	grandmother
238. 형제자매	sibling
239. 아버지	father
240. 어머니	mother
241. 동생	younger sibling
242. 여동생	younger sister (in general)
243. 남동생	younger brother (in general)
244. 누나	older sister (only used by boys)
245. 언니	older sister (only used by girls)
246. 형	older brother (only used by boys)
247. 오빠	older brother (only used by girls)
248. 사촌	cousin
249. 조카	nephew
250. 조카딸	niece

9 Vocabulary Activities

■ Word Match
Write the letter in the box next to the Korean word for the matching English.

> A. older sister (only used by boys)
> B. younger sister (in general)
> C. boyfriend
> D. nephew
> E. niece
> F. father
> G. girlfriend
> H. sibling
> I. older brother (only used by girls)
> J. older sister (only used by girls)
> K. boy, man
> L. cousin

☐ 조카딸   ☐ 여동생   ☐ 아버지
☐ 언니   ☐ 남자친구 ☐ 여자친구
☐ 남자   ☐ 누나   ☐ 조카
☐ 형제자매 ☐ 오빠   ☐ 사촌

■ Correct Korean
Choose the correct Korean for the English.

1. parents
A. 부옽님   B. 부오님   C. 부모김   D. 부모님

2. younger sibling
A. 동셍   B. 동셈   C. 동쟁   D. 동생

3. grandfather
A. 핱아버지 B. 할아버지 C. 할아버즌 D. 할아버짓

4. grandmother
A. 할머긴   B. 할머니   C. 할머느   D. 할맑니

5. mother
A. 어맑니   B. 어머기   C. 머머니   D. 어머니

9 Answer Key

■ Word Match (answers)

A. older sister (only used by boys)
B. younger sister (in general)
C. boyfriend
D. nephew
E. niece
F. father
G. girlfriend
H. sibling
I. older brother (only used by girls)
J. older sister (only used by girls)
K. boy, man
L. cousin

E	조카딸	B	여동생	F	아버지
J	언니	C	남자친구	G	여자친구
K	남자	A	누나	D	조카
H	형제자매	I	오빠	L	사촌

■ Correct Korean (answers)

1. **parents**
   A. 부욷님   B. 부오님   C. 부모김   **D. 부모님**

2. **younger sibling**
   A. 동셍   B. 동셈   C. 동쟁   **D. 동생**

3. **grandfather**
   A. 핟아버지   **B. 할아버지**   C. 할아버즌   D. 할아버짓

4. **grandmother**
   A. 할머긴   **B. 할머니**   C. 할머느   D. 할막니

5. **mother**
   A. 어막니   B. 어머기   C. 머머니   **D. 어머니**

9 Additional Writing Practice Area

232 남자	**231** 여자
234 남자친구	**233** 여자친구
236 할아버지	**235** 부모님
238 형제자매	**237** 할머니
240 어머니	**239** 아버지

231 girl, woman	232 boy, man
233 girlfriend	234 boyfriend
235 parents	236 grandfather
237 grandmother	238 sibling
239 father	240 mother

241	242
동생	여동생

243	244
남동생	누나

245	246
언니	형

247	248
오빠	사촌

249	250
조카	조카딸

241	242
younger sibling	younger sister (in general)

243	244
younger brother (in general)	older sister (only used by boys)

245	246
older sister (only used by girls)	older brother (only used by boys)

247	248
older brother (only used by girls)	cousin

249	250
nephew	niece

SOUTH KOREA
Provinces & Major Cities Map

대한민국

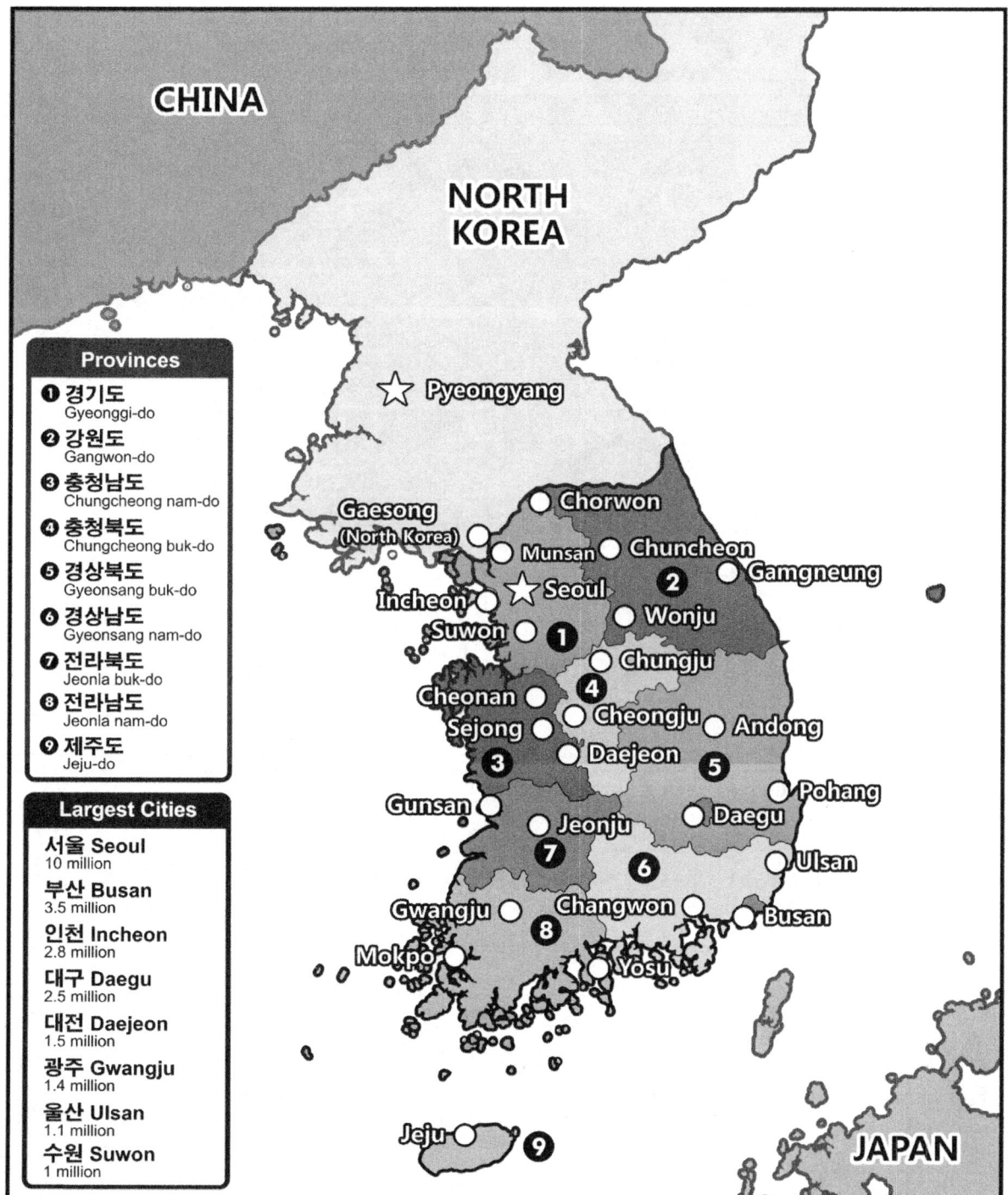

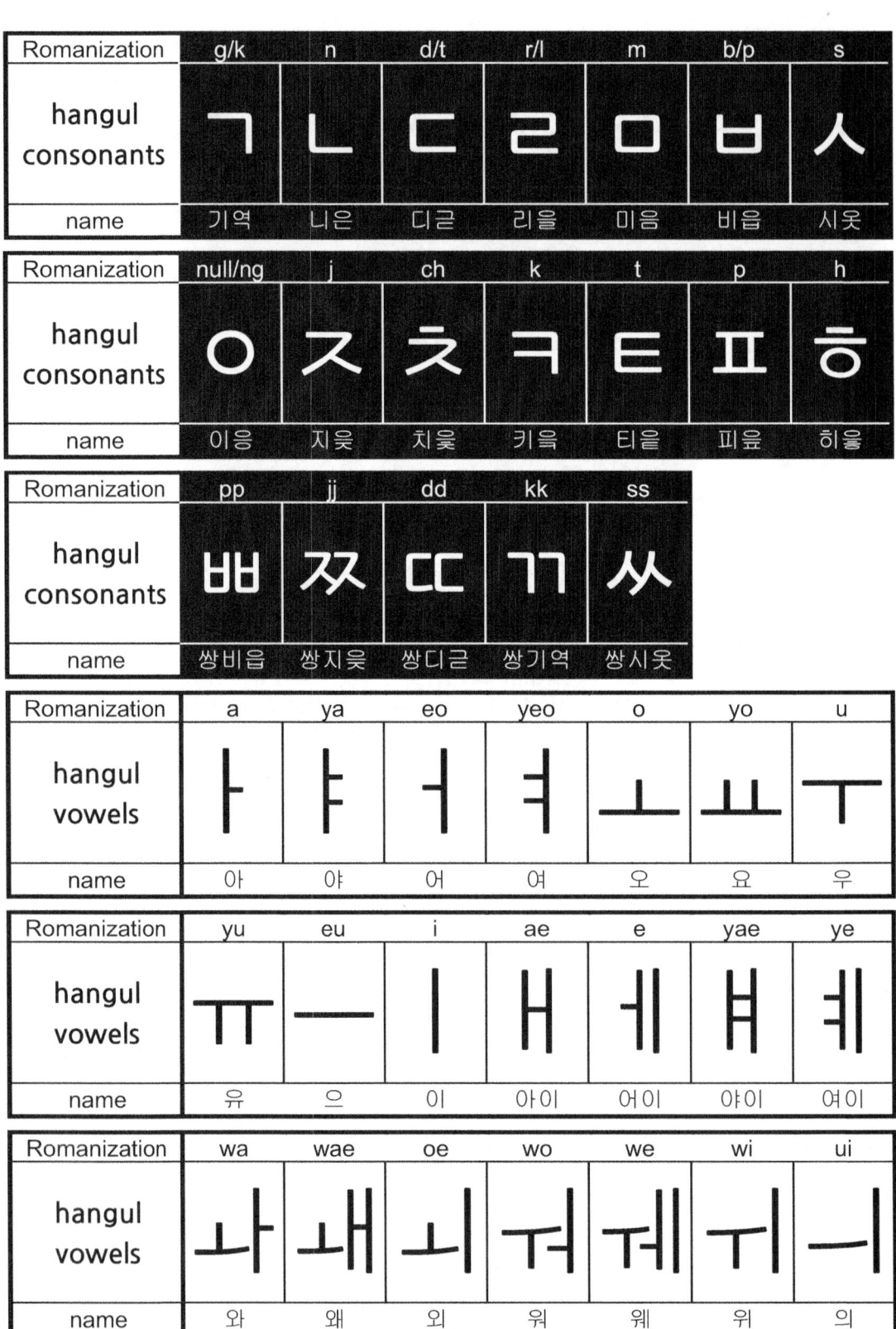

Cut out for reference.

Korean Keyboard Layout

© 2014 KoreanFromZero.com

Cut out for reference.

Korean Keyboard Layout

© 2014 KoreanFromZero.com

Other From Zero! Books

Printed in Dunstable, United Kingdom